Elizabeth Baird's
Classic Canadian Cooking

Menus for the Seasons

Elizabeth Baird's Classic Canadian Cooking

Menus for the Seasons

Anniversary Edition

Elizabeth Baird

James Lorimer & Company, Publishers   Toronto   1995

James Lorimer & Company Ltd. acknowledges with thanks the support of the Canada Council, the Ontario Arts Council and the Ontario Publishing Centre in the development of writing and publishing in Canada.

ISBN 1-55028-502-5
Cover photos: Douglas Bradshaw
Design: Lynn Campbell
Editing: Wayne Lawson

James Lorimer & Company, Publishers

Egerton Ryerson Memorial Building
35 Britain Street
Toronto

Printed and bound in Canada

Without the help of many people this book could not have been finished. My mother, Olive Davis, and my friends, Susan Carlton and Sandra Hall, helped in all stages of the book. Rachel van Nostrand generously lent her collection of cookbooks. Myfanwy Phillips and Jim Lorimer gave boundless encouragement. To all these people, my aunts, and the many friends who gave recipes, lent books, and helped with the testing and tasting, I would like to express my thanks.

E.B.

Cover Photos: Front, *Roast Loin of Pork with Thyme*, p.91; back left, *Scrambled Eggs*, p.44; back right, *Cranberry Muffins*, a variant of *Banana Muffins*, p.119.   Illustrations courtesy of the T. Eaton Co.

Contents

Preface to the Anniversary Edition

Twenty-one years have passed since the publication of *Classic Canadian Cooking, Menus for the Seasons*. This book opened the door for me to a rewarding career of exploring the diverse bounty of food in Canada.

This reprint offers the opportunity to look back at these two decades. Much is heartening on the Canadian food scene. A new generation of Canadian-trained chefs have been leaders in using Canadian seasonal produce and elevating what was essentially a home cooking tradition to a new level of deliciousness and sophistication. Notable among the many are Jamie Kennedy, currently at the Royal Ontario Museum in Toronto, Michael Olson who cooks up the bounty of the Niagara Peninsula at On-The-Twenty, Sinclair Philip's seafood extravaganza at Sooke Harbour House Inn on Vancouver Island, Anne Desjardins at L'Eau à la Bouche at Ste-Adèle, Quebec and Janet Palmer in Saskatoon.

A revival of farmers' markets in cities, towns and villages across the country has offered the opportunity for consumers and growers to get to know each other. The finest of these is the Granville Island Public Market where shoppers can buy Pacific salmon, fireweed honey, berries and hazelnuts from the Fraser Valley and the best selection of turkey anywhere in Canada. Nibbling and noshing are part of the scene, and the choices for sit-down snacking are as varied as Vietnamese salad rolls, sushi and souvlaki.

When the country doesn't come to the city, in the last twenty years the city has been going to the country. We can now go to "pick-your-own" farms and orchards where all the fun of harvesting can be had without the back-breaking planting and tending. City dwellers will find strawberries sweetened in the long summer sun's rays in Newfoundland's Humber Valley, delicious saskatoons in the Peace River Valley, vine-ripened tomatoes in Southwestern Ontario's heat belt around Windsor, and blueberries, the tasty, wild kind, to rake off the bushes in Nova Scotia and New Brunswick. If picking is not on the agenda, buying fresh is easy at numerous new country markets selling local produce. They are great destinations for pleasurable weekend drives.

Another wonderful development in the last twenty years is the emergence of great Canadian wines. What seemed a dream in 1974 is now a reality thanks to pioneers such as Donald Ziraldo of Ontario's Inniskillin Wines. Icewine showed the world that Canadian wines had award-winning potential, with rieslings, chardonnays and other red and white wines, astonishing and impressing judges and wine lovers alike. Also, the dozens of micro breweries have revived standards in brewing.

Equally encouraging is the emergence of a community of people and institutions who, for lack of a better expression, take pride in Canadian food. They are as diverse as Ann McColl, whose London, Ontario cookware shop would be hard to match anywhere; Carol Ferguson and Margaret Fraser, who put *Canadian Living* on the culinary map and consolidated the Canadian food tradition with *A Century of Canadian Home Cooking*; Bonnie Stern's fine cooking school; Toronto's Cookbook Store, not just a source of cookbooks but all matters culinary; The Taste of Nova Scotia, an organization that brings together agriculture, fisheries, restaurants and small food processors to promote and improve the food in that Atlantic province; restaurant critics, such as Marion Warhaft, Joanne Kates and Cynthia Wine, who keep everyone on their culinary toes; Anita Stewart whose dream of a cross-Canada culinary network has emerged as Cuisine Canada; James Morris and Eleanor Kane, Stratford Ontario restaurateurs and founders of the Stratford Chefs School; and raising the standards of chefs' training, journalists such as Julian Armstrong, who mapped out the good cooking in Quebec, Judy Schultz in Edmonton and *City Food's* creator Rhonda May in Vancouver; Noel Richardson, who grows herbs on Vancouver Island; David Cohlmeyer, who has a passion for the land and the organic vegetables he grows; and so many more people it's impossible to name them all. And there is the equally important community of the thousands of people who care about the food they buy, care about how they cook it and care about their families and guests who sit down at the table to enjoy it.

Canadian cuisine has also experienced losses in the last twenty years, some of them very serious — such as the tragic disappearance of the East Coast cod fishery and the serious threat posed to wild salmon on both coasts. We have lost varieties of fruit and vegetables that don't ship well or have short shelf lives. Cooking instruction in schools is disappearing. Industrialized food growing and processing blunt the nuances of taste. For too many of us, overwork and stress cut into the time we spend planning, cooking and sitting down together to build culinary memories and traditions. But, just as over the past twenty years unforeseen improvements emerged on the Canadian food scene, so there is room for optimism for the future. Please enjoy this slice of Canadiana with good appetite and good cheer.

Elizabeth Baird
July 1995

Introduction

This book is a compendium of what I consider to be the best of Canadian cooking. I hope it will undo an underlying conditioning in many of us to regard Canadian cooking as a rather boring, unsophisticated cuisine.

The recipes are of three basic types. First, there are the best possible renditions of such classic dishes as rhubarb pie, chili sauce, plum pudding, roast duck, and roast beef. Second, there are dishes distinguished by the unusual use of native products, such as winter squash and rose water pudding, pumpkin soup, spiced beef, scripture cake, and royal strawberry acid. Third, there are dishes that were once well-known but that have been forgotten, either because of lack of interest in Canadian cooking or because of the development of new technologies and products which have pushed these older recipes aside; these include old-fashioned trifle, gooseberry fool, real baked ham, dried apple cake, Jerusalem artichokes, Indian pudding, and iced maple mousse.

Any contemporary book that relies on the heritage of Canadian cooking for its recipes is bound to provide a link with the past, but I hope this one will do more than that. For in examining the inventive foods made by this country's early cooks in response to the seasonal cycle, we may actually discover new, tempting, elegant dishes with which to take special advantage still of the produce of the country and the seasons of the year. So it isn't just in search of our ancestors that we should turn to Canadian cooking; it is in search of fine new dishes and inventive variations on familiar ones.

The recipes in this book are organized into menus according to the season when their principal ingredients are fresh and at their prime. Because modern transport, freezing, and storage facilities make many foods available year round, we tend to lose our sense of the seasons. This is especially true for people who have to shop in supermarkets. But food harvested before it is mature in order to survive lengthy shipping is never as good as fresh, local produce. Moreover, when local crops are at their prime, prices are at their lowest, and while very few of us can afford to eat fresh sweet cherries in mid-winter, all of us can enjoy them in early summer. Just by following the rhythm of the seasons, we can turn unmatchable Canadian produce into elegant Canadian cooking.

By classic Canadian cooking, I mean the Upper Canadian cooking tradition evolved in the 1800's and early 1900's. Upper Canadian cooking is somewhat different from East Coast cooking and substantially different from Quebecois cooking.

What are now the Maritime Provinces were settled much earlier than Upper Canada and were for a long time colonies quite separate from the Canadas. The range of local produce was in many ways similar to what was available in Upper Canada, but there were important differences too, particularly in the realm of seafood. Settlers in the Maritimes arrived with the same background in Scottish, Irish, English, and American cooking as those who arrived later in Upper Canada, though it was New Englanders who came to the Maritimes and residents of Pennsylvania and New York who arrived in Upper Canada. The French influence was strong on the East Coast and sea links provided constant direct contact with Europe and the United States, whereas Upper Canada was cut off. These circumstances made it easier for the East Coast to follow more closely the cooking of the mother country, whereas the Upper Canadians were forced to rely more on what they had available locally and what their own ingenuity could devise out of it. Their location on the sea gave the Maritimes a fantastic range of fish and shellfish, which made their diet and their cooking quite different from that of Upper Canada.

Nevertheless, similar ethnic backgrounds and local produce effected close parallels in the two cooking traditions. Many dishes are shared, for instance cucumbers in sour cream, steamed brown bread, shortbread, gingerbread cookies, raspberry vinegar, cream of potato soup, and many dishes featuring molasses and oatmeal. *Out of Old Nova Scotia Kitchens*, the most comprehensive book available on East Coast cookery, presents the best of these.

Meanwhile a separate and very distinguished cooking style

was being developed in Quebec. Based on the peasant French cooking tradition brought to this country 360 years ago and adapted to suit the rigorous climate and new Canadian ingredients, and having in addition a strain of classical bourgeois French cooking, there was an emphasis on careful cooking, quality of ingredients, and tradition which remains strong in Quebec to this day. Pork cooked in a tremendous variety of ways, dishes featuring maple products and apples, game, and seafood are outstanding features of Quebecois cooking and have been recorded in many cookbooks both specialized and general.

If, therefore, the term "classic Canadian cooking" seems too broad for the tradition presented in this book, it is still, I think, the best short descriptive phrase for it. "Ontario cooking" would be too narrow, because the tradition has been developed and is known over a much wider area of the country. East Coast cooks would not use the term "Canadian" to describe their cooking tradition, nor would the cooks of Quebec. Almost by default, then, this is the cooking style which seems best suited to be termed "Canadian."

With its concentration on the central tradition of Upper Canadian cooking, the framework of this book does not allow room for the separate and very diverse ethnic cooking traditions which survive and prosper across this country. One great advantage of the existence of these national cuisines side by side is that it is easy for all of us to cook Chinese, Italian, Scandinavian, and East European dishes with ingredients and produce that are often fresh and easily available. In earlier times, similar influences—particularly of German settlers in Ontario—were felt on the classic Canadian tradition. Those influences are obvious in many of the recipes presented here.

My research for the recipes in this book led me to all kinds of sources: printed cookbooks dating from 1831 right up to the present, local women's groups' collections of recipes, handwritten personal collections, newspapers, magazines, pamphlets, libraries, and innumerable private kitchens. The resulting menus are all based on these sources, often adapted to modern ingredients and techniques.

The book is divided into four sections according to the seasons. For each season there are menus principally for dinners, but also for suppers, lunches, breakfasts, and teas. The majority are meant to be "special" meals, for example Christmas and New Year's, but I have included as well some casual suppers, picnics, and barbecues. Preserves are in a section by themselves at the back of the book. So are a small number of basic recipes such as pie crust and mayonnaise.

Many menus offer one choice for each course, as one might expect in a menu cookbook. However, in some cases such as apple desserts, fruit pies, sherbets, and ice creams, the possibilities are so numerous that more than one choice has been offered. When this occurs, picking the recipe becomes a matter of individual taste, availability of produce, and creativity. As much as possible, I have tried to maintain an overall texture, colour, and taste balance no matter which choice is made, while still offering a broad representative selection of recipes

The drinking of table wine in Canada has increased dramatically since the 1940's. British Columbia and New Brunswick both produce fruit wines, and Ontario's Niagara Peninsula produces grape wine. Conflicting reasons are offered to explain why Niagara wine is not superior table wine. Some people argue that the climate will not permit the growth of the sort of grapes necessary to make wines of European quality. Others suggest that the industry is at fault inasmuch as it is gearing its product not to serious table wine but rather to a more lucrative market specializing in fizzy, sweet, soft-drink wines. Whatever the reason, I have not suggested specific Canadian wines for the menus in this book.

Canadian beer, on the other hand, is excellent. It ranges from mild malt lagers to nicely fragrant hop-flavoured ale. It's a very good accompaniment to many of the menus in this book.

Apple cider is a fine, old-time Canadian drink. In the days of local cider mills, there was a short-lived abundance of natural sweet cider. Little of this local cider is now produced. However, the Quebec Liquor Board currently markets excellent hard ciders produced in the Rougemont area, and these are recommended for some meals. Cider is also excellent for cooking purposes, replacing wine. Unfortunately, some provincial liquor boards are dragging their heels in making Quebec cider available across the country.

How to Use This Book

There are several ways. One is to look up the appropriate season, find a menu that suits your occasion, and prepare the dishes in the menu. All the necessary instructions for each dish in the meal except preserves and a few basic recipes are together. Some menus have one choice for each course while others may have three or four choices for a course. In these cases, choose whichever recipe appeals to you most.

Another way to use the book is to go to the index, say for a recipe for peaches, and find there all the recipes in the book for peaches: in chutney, as a sherbet, in fruit salad, or in pie. Similarly, you can look under the index entry for pie and find peach pie, as well as maple syrup, raspberry cream, and all the others. That is to say, the index is organized by the type of dish and principal ingredient to facilitate use of the book.

Any of the menus can be varied by interchanging dishes from other menus; and of course, any dish can be cooked to fit in with your own menus.

All the dinner menus have a starter, usually a soup but occasionally an hors d'oeuvre, then a main course of meat, fish, or shellfish, a vegetable, salad, and dessert. An appropriate beverage is usually indicated to serve as a rough guide. Suppers do not include a starter, and especially in the winter ones, greater use is made of pickles and relishes than of salads.

The index includes a guide to recipes which are time-consuming, which can be prepared in advance and which can easily be prepared. Three symbols are used: * indicates a recipe requiring some time to cook; + indicates that the recipe can be made in advance; 0 indicates a quick and easy recipe.

All the recipes are for 6 persons unless otherwise indicated.

Measurements are by volume: 1 cup = 8 fluid ounces. Pints and quarts are the imperial measure: 1 pint = 20 ounces (2 ½ cups), 1 quart = 40 ounces (5 cups).

Where a time is specified, for example, "simmer 10 minutes," there is also a description of how the food should look at the end of that time, because variations of saucepan size and thickness, stoves, weather, and ingredients can all influence how a recipe turns out. Nevertheless, it is assumed that all produce will be very fresh and of the highest quality.

The recipes vary in cost, with the main course generally the most expensive item. However, the use of fruits and vegetables in season and the habit of making your own pastries, cakes, and breads will offset what may appear to be expensive meals.

In these menus I have operated on the premise that all items will be made from scratch—bread, stocks, sauces, pickles, etc. Where this is not applicable, substitute only top-quality store-bought goods.

A Little Historical Background

The first "Canadian" cookbook appeared in 1831. Its full title was *The Cook Not Mad or Rational Cookery—Being a collection of original and selected Recipes, embracing not only the art of curing various kinds of Meats and Vegetables for future use, but of Cooking, in its general acceptance to the taste, habits and degrees of luxury, prevalent with the Canadian Public.* Though published in Kingston, Canada West, it was in fact an American cookbook, including such obvious patriotic fare as Washington Cake, Federal Cake, and Jackson Jumbles. Nevertheless, many of its recipes were useful, especially those for curing meats and preserving fruits and vegetables. No. 3 tells how "To pickle one hundred pounds of Beef to keep a year" and No. 202 how "To preserve plums and cherries, six months or a year, retaining all that bloom and agreeable flavour during the whole of that period, of which they are possessed when taken from a tree." The book relies considerably on North American ingredients, as can be seen in the recipes for "crookneck or winter squash Pudding," "Pompion Pudding," and "Buckwheat cakes". Six recipes for pastry indicate an early interest in both savoury and sweet fruit pies. There are also numerous recipes for doughnuts, puddings, cakes, and cookies. While this book may not have been useful to settlers eking out a subsistence in their first few years in the bush, it could well have been appreciated by Canadian families in more established areas.

A number of technological advances of the 1830's and 40's did much to improve Canadian cookery. The most important was the development and distribution of the cookstove. Stoves had been used for heating in the eighteenth century, but it wasn't until the mid-nineteenth century that they were widely used for cooking in Canada. No more did the cook have to manipulate complicated spits, pulleys, and chains before an open fireplace, and there was much less heavy lifting, because stove cooking was done at a comfortable waist level. The stove was also clean and reliable and it was easy to regulate the temperature of both the oven and the top cooking surfaces. Efficient ovens assured good bread, cakes, and pies, and no doubt encouraged roasting as a method of cooking meat. Cooking on a stove could also be done in greater quantities than in a fireplace. A variety of cooking methods could go on simultaneously; for example, a pudding could be steamed over moderate heat while soup simmered at the back of the stove, and while meat roasted in the oven, warming or drying of food could go on over the stove.

Contemporary with the stove was a whole range of what were termed Yankee cooking gadgets including matches, cistern pumps, sausage stuffers, zinc sinks, apple corers, cherry pitters and lemon squeezers, which made the production of large quantities of food much easier.

Meanwhile, new farm machinery increased the size of crops, and nursery seeds improved their quality. Also, railways and steamship lines made transportation of foodstuffs easier, until once terribly expensive products were available to many. The arrival of sugar and molasses from the West Indies coincided luckily with a growing abundance of food, new knowledge of sterilization and food preservation, and the production of cheap glass. The first glass Mason jar of 1858 revolutionized the making of jams, jellies, relishes, and pickles. As seafood from the coast became available inland, oysters were eventually called for by "half a hundred" in Upper Canadian recipes.

Cookbooks of the 40's, 50's, and 60's reflected this economic expansion. In 1845, *Modern Cookery*, written by Mrs. Nourse, a native of Edinburgh, was published in both Kingston and Hamilton. Including such international recipes as Soup Cressey, Maintenant chops, and curries, *Modern Cookery* was fundamentally an English-Scottish cookbook for the middle class. Nevertheless, the fact that such a book could be published in Canada in 1845 indicates an early market for sophisticated cooking. This book and other English-style recipe books—notably Mrs. Beeton's monumental *Household Management of 1861*—reinforced a tradition still found in Canadian cooking—the tradition of plum puddings, fruit cakes, Yorkshire puddings, custards, and trifles.

Miss Beecher's 1842 *Treatise on Domestic Economy* and her *Domestic Receipt Book* of 1854 published in New York were one source of a continuing American influence on Canadian cooking and homemaking. Four other American cookbooks, *The Frugal Housewife* by Mrs. Child, the *House Book* and *Receipt Book* by Miss Eliza Leslie, and the 1859 edition of *The Family and Housekeeper's Guide*, strengthened the Canadian-American link in cooking. Miss Beecher's 1854 book contains many basic items such as bread, yeast, and cheese making plus such fancy recipes as Wine Cake, Brandied Peaches, and Spiced Chocolate. Her recipe for Royal Strawberry Acid found its way 30 years later into a handwritten recipe book in Hamilton—evidence that the book continued to be well used.

The *Canadian Housewife's Manual of Cookery*, published in Hamilton in 1861, is perhaps the most Canadian cookbook of this period. The editor notes that it is "carefully compiled from the best English, French, and American Works—especially adapted to this country."

In content and moral tone, it owes much to Eliza Acton, the English author of *The Modern Housewife* (1845), and to Alexis Soyer, a well-known French cookbook writer and chef living at that time in London. There is, however, a new stress on native Canadian vegetables, with recipes for squash, pumpkins, and especially tomatoes. Fourteen recipes in all encourage the use of tomatoes: stuffed, with sweetbreads, scalloped, stewed, in soup, fried with ham, preserved, in sauce, as catsup, pickled, and dried! Although there are expensive recipes in the book, the overall tone is one of sensible economy. The book enjoins the housewife "to make home the sweet refuge of a husband fatigued by intercourse with a jarring world."

By about 1870, technology, improved transportation, and the growth of commercial cities had all conspired to make cooking in Canada a more refined and leisurely undertaking. Nevertheless, there remained both in urban and rural Canadian communities a deep-down sense of season—of the "right" time to eat strawberries or blueberries or trout or pork. All over the country, bees, festivals, and parties were the pleasant rituals that grew out of strawberry picking, apple harvesting, and smelt fishing. And always in the back of the mind was the accompanying economic urge to preserve some of this abundance for the cold winter. Cookbooks of the late nineteenth century and early twentieth century reflect this pattern. *The Canadian Home Cook Book* of 1877 has 50 recipes for pickles and relish and 36 for preserves, jams, and jellies. *The New Galt Cook Book, A Manual of Cookery and Domestic Economy* (1908) has whole encyclopaedic sections on the preservation of fruits and vegetables.

In cookbooks of this period there is also an astounding profusion of recipes for cakes, puddings, cookies, and pies. Especially from old personal recipe collections, one might get the impression that Canadians ate only jams, jellies, pickles, relishes, cakes, pies, puddings, and perhaps a few platefuls of oyster fricassee or stew. The 1877 *Canadian Home Cook Book*, compiled by the Ladies of Toronto and other chief cities and towns in Canada, contains no fewer than 105 recipes for cakes and cookies and 84 for puddings. Once the West opened up and the world's finest grain was available cheap to all Canadians, there seemed to be no limit to the ingenuity cooks used in creating sweets and desserts. Cakes ranged in the 1915 *Red Roses Cook Book* from the regular Fudge Cake, Oatmeal Cake, and Ribbon Cake to such specialties as Scriptural Cake, Pork Fruit Cake, Pepper Cake, Hickory Nut Cake, and Manitoba Black Cake.

For the next 70 years or so, all over Canada, women were cooking up a storm. Local cookbooks compiled by church groups, women's institutes, sewing circles, and schools proliferated. All these books reflect tremendous pride in fancy preserving, pickling, and baking. There are surprisingly few recipes for roasting meats, making stews and soups, or preparing vegetables. The assumption seems to be that women just naturally know how to prepare this basic repertoire of dishes using the freshest, best ingredients. All they need or want written down are preserving, pickling, and baking recipes. Such were the recipes that made a cook's name. The pies, cakes, cookies, and preserves she brought to a church supper, a funeral, a fall fair, a wedding, or a family picnic could make or break a woman's reputation.

Right up to the Second World War, then, one could confidently say that there was a Canadian style of cooking based largely on foods grown in Canada. Since then, however, a number of factors have led to the decline of that cooking tradition. These factors include rapid urbanization, the move for women to work outside the home, the tendency to import more and more food, the practice of selling more and more food partly or wholly processed, the loss of locally responsive merchants through the monopolization of food retailing by supermarkets, a sharp decline in home gardening, the gradual loss of a host of small local industries producing quality cider, flour, cheese, and meat products, and the accompanying rise of giant international corporations. Gradually, since the Second World War, a uniform, bland taste, glorified on mass media and profitable to the food companies, has inserted itself in our national diet.

Before we forget that there ever was such a thing as old-time Canadian cooking, we should stop and consider its strengths. First, there was a respect in it for the Canadian land and the fruits of it. Second, there was a rhythm to it as rich and fluid as the seasonal cycle. Third, there was a pride about it in the sheer savvy of excellence, manifested in a succulent roast, a crisp pickle, a made-from-scratch Christmas pudding, or a mouth-watering strawberry shortcake. Surely these are strengths we should be reluctant to lose.

Spring

"Will spring *ever* come? When I look out upon the bleak, shrouded, changeless scene, there is something so awfully silent, fixed, and immutable in its aspect, that it is enough to disturb one's faith in the everlasting revolutions of the seasons. Green leaves and flowers, and streams that murmur as they flow, soft summer airs, to which we open the panting bosom—panting with too much life—shades grateful for their coolness—can such things be, or do they exist only in Poetry and Paradise?" (Anna Brownell Jameson, *Winter Studies and Summer Rambles in Canada.*)

Writing in Toronto in 1837, Mrs. Jameson was not the first Canadian resident to long for spring, nor will she be the last. Her passionate intensity may be more understandable to us, however, if we imagine what nineteenth-century cooking and housekeeping must have entailed. By March, the remaining fruits and vegetables stored in her root cellar had begun to turn soft or to sprout, her supply of preserved or dried fruits and vegetables was running short, and the taste of salted and pickled meats and fish had certainly begun to pall. Any signs of spring must have been welcome.

The first of these in many parts of Canada was the maple sugar season in March. Though this meant cold days and nights in the sugar shanty, early settlers looked forward to the work, which provided the sole supply of sweetening for most tables. Cane sugar was too expensive and honey required more time and skill to produce.

In general, maple sugar was considered preferable to maple syrup. The sugar was easier to keep and required fewer containers, and the syrup, or molasses as many English Canadians called it, got mouldy if it was not tightly sealed. The syrup gave Mrs. Jameson one more cause for complaint; in describing maple molasses, she moans, "I shall get used [to it] in time—I must try, at least, or thank Heaven, fasting." For her contemporary

Catherine Parr Traill, on the other hand, it formed "a nice ingredient in cakes, and an excellent sauce for puddings." Mrs. Traill sent the following description of the sugaring process to her family in England:

> It was a pretty and picturesque sight to see the sugar-boilers, with their bright log-fire among the trees, now stirring up the blazing pile, now throwing in the liquid and stirring it down with a big ladle. When the fire grew fierce, it boiled and foamed up in the kettle, and they had to throw in fresh sap to keep it from running over.
>
> When the sap begins to thicken into molasses it is then brought to the sugar-boiler to be finished. The process is simple; it only requires attention in skimming and keeping the mass from boiling over till it has arrived at the sugaring point, which is ascertained by dropping a little in cold water. When it is near the proper consistency, the kettle or pot becomes full of yellow froth that dimples and rises in large bubbles from beneath. These throw out puffs of steam, and when the molasses is in this stage, it is nearly converted into sugar. Those who pay great attention to keep the liquid free from scum, and understand the precise sugaring point, will produce an article little if at all inferior to muscovado.

The peak of the maple season was the sugaring-off parties held in the maple camp. Syrup boiled almost to the hard sugar point and poured onto fresh, clean snow formed delicious chewy pieces that were considered a real treat.

The late April sap was made into maple vinegar. The sap was boiled down from five gallons to one, set to ferment in a warm place, and used for late summer pickling.

By May, Mrs. Jameson's fondest prayers for leaves and flowers and streams that murmur would be answered. In the bush and fields was a profusion of wild leeks, asparagus, tender dandelion leaves, fiddleheads, flowers, gooseberries, and strawberries. The streams brimmed with watercress and the finest trout. For Canadians close to the Great Lakes, smelts were always plentiful in spring. A few warm nights bring millions of these small fish close to the shoreline as they go to spawn in the creeks and rivers. When the smelt were "running", fishermen could scoop them up with a basket. Smaller lakes to the north yielded maskinonge, salmon-trout, pickerel, pike, and bass. Even salmon, now found only in British Columbia and the Maritimes, was common in Ontario.

Spring also meant ham. When farmers butchered pigs in late November, they salted down most of the meat in barrels or made it into sausages. They gave only the choicest pieces, the hams and shoulders, the extra treatment of curing in brine followed by smoking. These they often reserved for special occasions such as Easter Sunday.

By May, ploughing, sowing, and planting went on incessantly: "No time for the gardener or husbandman to be idle," as Mrs. Traill points out in her *Female Emigrants' Guide*.

The cycle of garden produce is the same now as it was 140 years ago, but because of the presence of so many imported products, especially fruits and vegetables, the cycle is blurred. For example, asparagus shipped in from the United States is on sale in most of Canada two months before homegrown asparagus is available. If spring with its array of subtle fresh flavours therefore seems less momentous to us than it did to Mrs. Jameson, it is because we have replaced the natural sequence of really tasty fresh food with a profusion of expensive imported food that is usually of inferior quality.

Rhubarb, chives, winter onions, and asparagus are still the first Canadian crops from the garden. By June, leaf lettuce, radishes, strawberries, and green peas come into season. The gamble involved in gardening is the same now as in 1830. If you plant early, you will reap early, but you still run the risk of having frost or continued wet weather wipe out everything.

Our best spring food remains our own native products—asparagus fresh from the garden, wild or cultivated strawberries, pungent wild leeks from the bush, the first leaf lettuce salad, the just-caught speckled trout. Many of these are featured in the recipes which follow.

Tarragon Spring Chicken
with
Mushroom and Wine Sauce

Cheddar Cheese Soup

Tarragon Spring Chicken with Mushroom and Wine Sauce
Steamed New Potatoes in Buttered Herbs

Cos Lettuce Salad

Floating Island

Suggested wine:
dry red or chilled white

Cheddar cheese, originally from the village of Cheddar near Bristol in England, was brought to Canada by the Loyalists. All Ontario cheese was made in farmhouses until 1864, when the first cheese factory was built in Ingersoll. Before long, good agricultural land was sprinkled with local cheese factories, all producing cheddar but, naturally, each imparting its own individual taste to the cheese. Most of these small factories have had to shut down in recent years as giant corporations, particularly Kraft, have taken over the Canadian cheese industry.

The cos lettuce salad (romaine is the name now commonly applied to this long crisp lettuce) comes from the *Manual of Cookery* (1861), the most sophisticated nineteenth-century Canadian cookbook. It has an oil and vinegar dressing in the French style. The salad section in the *Manual of Cookery* is unlike that in other Canadian cookbooks of the period, in that it contains recipes for salads made from fish, cos lettuce, cabbage lettuce, dandelion, endive, marshmallow, mustard, cress, and beetroot instead of the usual salads of the time—chicken, potato, and cabbage. The dressing for these salads is an oil and vinegar dressing, but a most interesting feature is the use of chervil, tarragon, chives, or even garlic in the dressing. The author does concede that adding garlic puts a salad in the French tradition.

¼ cup butter
⅓ cup minced onion
⅓ cup grated carrot
2 tbsp flour
3 cups lightly salted chicken
   stock (see basic recipes)
½ tsp dry mustard
½ tsp paprika
1 ¼ cups light cream
1 ½ cups grated cheddar
   cheese (½ lb)
1 cup ale

Cheddar Cheese Soup

Melt the butter in a saucepan. Add the onion and carrot. Cover and cook over low heat 5 minutes. Stir in the flour. Continue cooking 3-4 minutes, gradually adding the stock and stirring all the time. Add the mustard and paprika. Simmer 20-25 minutes or until the vegetables are tender. (For a smooth soup, it may now be blended or passed through a sieve.) Add the cream, cheese, and ale. Simmer until the soup is heated through and the cheese is melted. Stir constantly.

6 large chicken breasts or two
   2-lb broilers, quartered
6 tbsp butter, melted
2 tbsp lemon juice
1 tsp dry mustard
1 tsp chopped fresh tarragon
   (½ tsp dried crushed)
¼ tsp freshly ground pepper
½ tsp salt for underside of the
   chicken
½ tsp salt for skin side of the
   chicken

Sauce:
pan juices
2 cups very finely chopped
   mushrooms
½ cup finely chopped green
   onions
¼ tsp salt
⅛ tsp freshly ground pepper
2 tsp cornstarch
1 tsp soft butter
3 tbsp white wine
1 tsp chopped fresh tarragon
   (½ tsp dried crushed)
1 tsp lemon juice

Tarragon Spring Chicken with Mushroom and Wine Sauce

Lay the chicken skin side down in a broiler tray. Combine the melted butter, lemon juice, mustard, 1 tsp tarragon, and ¼ tsp pepper and brush over the chicken parts. Grill 5"-6" from the heat surface for 10 minutes, basting once during this period with the melted butter mixture. Salt the underside, turn, and grill skin side up, basting every 5 minutes with the melted butter mixture until the chicken is tender but not overcooked. The breasts will take about 8-10 minutes on this side, and drumstick quarters up to about 15 minutes. To test for doneness, prick the chicken at its thickest part. If the juice runs clear and yellow, the chicken is done. Salt the skin side.

Remove the chicken to a preheated platter. To prepare the sauce, add the mushrooms, onions, salt, and pepper to the accumulated juices in the broiling pan and froth up to quickly cook the vegetables. Mix the cornstarch and butter to a paste and work into the vegetables. Add the wine. Cook 1-2 minutes, then stir in the tarragon and lemon juice, and pour over the chicken. Serve immediately.

Steamed New Potatoes in Buttered Herbs

12-18 small new potatoes
½ tsp sea salt
¼ cup butter, melted
3 tbsp finely chopped parsley
½ tsp finely chopped fresh dill
¼ tsp grated lemon rind

Scrub the potatoes with a stiff brush to remove the skins. Place in a steamer over boiling water, cover, and steam 20-25 minutes or until tender. Shake with the salt over heat to dry. Place potatoes in a preheated serving dish, pour over the butter, and toss gently to coat all the potatoes. Sprinkle on the parsley, dill, and lemon rind. Shake gently to distribute the herbs and lemon rind.

Cos Lettuce Salad

1 medium head cos lettuce
(now called romaine)

Dressing:
⅓ cup olive oil
1½ tbsp red wine vinegar
1 clove garlic, crushed
½ tsp salt
¼ tsp freshly ground pepper
1 tsp finely chopped fresh
chervil (½ tsp dried crushed)
½ tsp finely chopped fresh
tarragon (¼ tsp dried
crushed)
1 tbsp finely chopped fresh
chives

Separate the lettuce leaves. Wash and dry them thoroughly. Wrap in a damp tea towel and put in a plastic bag. Chill in the refrigerator 1-2 hours. Combine the ingredients for the dressing in a glass jar and shake well. Break the big leaves into bite-sized pieces in the centre of a salad bowl. Arrange the small, tender, light green leaves upright around the edge. Pour the dressing evenly over the leaves. Serve.

4 egg yolks
5 tbsp white sugar
⅛ tsp salt
3 egg whites
5 tbsp white sugar
1 cup light cream
1 ½ cups milk
1 ½″ piece of vanilla bean

Garnish:
½ cup sugar

Floating Island

Beat the yolks, first 5 tbsp sugar, and salt together. Reserve. Beat the whites until they are not quite stiff. Beat in the second 5 tbsp sugar gradually. Heat the cream, milk, and vanilla bean together in a flat wide pan to just below boiling point.

Using 2 large spoons, form the egg white mixture into 6 smooth oval shapes.

Poach the ovals 3 at a time in the just simmering cream and milk, 2 minutes on each side. Drain on a piece of paper towel.

Put the egg yolks, sugar, and salt into the top of a double boiler. Strain the cream and milk mixture into the yolks and place over barely simmering water. Stir well. Cook until the mixture just coats a spoon (165 degrees). Pour the custard into a low, preferably clear, glass dish. Arrange the ovals on the top.

Slowly melt the ½ cup sugar over medium heat. Cook until it is slightly caramelized. Pull threads of this over the custard and eggs. Cool.

Herbed Leg of Lamb Dinner

Atlantic Fish Chowder

Herbed Leg of Lamb with Mint-Apple Jelly Sauce
Buttered New Peas and Lettuce

Dandelion Salad with Bacon and Sour Cream Dressing

Rhubarb Custard Meringue Pie
or
Classic Double-crust Rhubarb Pie

Suggested wine:
dry red

Ideally, Atlantic fish chowder is made with fresh fillets of halibut, haddock, cod, and sole, but any combination of these firm-fleshed whitefish or even any of them alone produces a good chowder, and the addition of a few fresh shrimps, while not altogether following the Canadian tradition, gives the chowder extra colour, texture, and flavour. It is important not to overcook the chowder. The cubes of potato, the chopped onion, and the leeks should be tender, the fish ready to flake, and the stock full of flavour and creamy. If the soup is overcooked, the vegetables become mushy, the fish falls apart, and the liquid loses its distinct quality.

The recipe for the buttered new peas and lettuce comes from the *Manual of Cookery* and shows the French influence at work. This is a combination of the tenderest, greenest garden vegetables, new peas, lettuce, and green onions, simmered in butter with a suggestion of sugar. If possible, cook and serve the peas in the same fireproof dish so as not to disturb the nest of lettuce leaves lining the dish.

Dandelion is a salad ingredient much appreciated by the Amish and Mennonite communities. If the dandelion is covered with straw as it grows, the resulting bleached leaves will be tenderer and less bitter. The bacon and sour cream dressing used here is one popular in the Kitchener-Waterloo area of Ontario.

For dessert, there are two rhubarb pie recipes. The rhubarb custard meringue is a delicious combination of creamy and tart, and looks quite sensational with its peaked meringue. For purists, I am including the best recipe I have found for the classic, two-crusted pie.

Atlantic Fish Chowder

2 tbsp butter
1 cup chopped leeks (1 medium, white part only)
⅔ cup chopped onions
1 ⅓ cups diced, peeled potatoes (2 medium)
1 tbsp flour
1 ½ lbs fillets of cod, sole, halibut, or haddock
4 cups fish stock (see below)
1 ½ tsp salt
½ tsp freshly ground pepper
2 slices bacon
¼ lb small cooked shrimps
1 cup milk
1 cup medium or heavy cream
1 tbsp butter

Melt the 2 tbsp butter in a large, heavy-bottomed saucepan. Add the leeks and onions, stir to coat, and cook 4 minutes over moderate heat. Stir in the potatoes and cook 1 minute, covered. Mix in the flour, coating all the vegetables thoroughly.

Cut the fish fillets into ¾" pieces. Add to the vegetables, cook 1 minute. Pour in the stock, salt, and pepper, stirring well to prevent lumps.

Cut the bacon into ½" pieces. Bring it to the boil in a separate saucepan in water to cover. Drain off the water, and add the bacon to the chowder. Bring the chowder to the boil, reduce heat, and simmer 20 minutes. Do not overcook or the fish will disintegrate. Slice the shrimps in half lengthwise and add to the chowder just at the end of the cooking time. Scald the milk and cream together. Combine with the chowder. Taste, correct seasoning. Pour into a tureen, swirl in the 1 tbsp butter, serve.

Fish Stock for Chowder

1 tbsp butter
¼ cup chopped onions
½ cup chopped leeks
1 ½ lbs fish scraps, bones, heads
2 stalks parsley
⅛ tsp dill seed
½ bay leaf
⅛ tsp dried crushed thyme (¼ tsp chopped fresh)
3 peppercorns
½ tsp salt
5 cups cold water

Melt the butter, add the vegetables, and cook covered 1-2 minutes over low heat. Add the fish scraps, bones and heads, cover and cook 2 more minutes. Add the rest of the ingredients. Bring to the boil, reduce heat, and simmer uncovered 25-30 minutes. Do not overcook or the stock will be bitter. Strain immediately through a fine sieve. Yield: 4-5 cups.

Herbed Leg of Lamb

1 leg of lamb, 4-6 lbs
¼ lemon
¾ tsp dried crushed rosemary
    or 1 ½ tsp fresh chopped
    rosemary
1 tbsp dry mustard
½ tsp ground ginger
¼ tsp freshly ground pepper
1 large clove garlic, crushed
3 tbsp oil
1 tsp salt

Sauce (optional):
1 cup beef stock (see basic
    recipes)
1 tbsp mint-apple jelly (see
    preserves section)
¼ tsp salt

Wipe the leg with a damp cloth. Rub all over with the lemon. Set on a rack in an open roasting pan. Combine all the rest of the ingredients except the salt in a bowl and mash together. Brush or spoon all over the lamb. Let stand 2 hours at room temperature to absorb the flavours.

Roast at 350 degrees for 20-25 minutes per pound. For rare, internal temperature should be 160 degrees; for medium 170 degrees; and for well done 180 degrees. Rare and medium settings give the juiciest roast. Remove from the oven. Sprinkle on the salt and place on a preheated platter in a warm place for 20 minutes. This sets the roast by allowing the juices to flow back into the tissue, and makes it easier to carve.

If a sauce is desired, skim fat from the pan, add 1 cup stock to the remaining juices, and boil up 2-3 minutes, stirring and scraping up all the crusty bits. Then add the jelly and salt. Taste, add more salt if desired. Simmer 3-4 minutes, adding any juices that have dripped from the roast. Serve in a preheated gravy boat.

Buttered New Peas and Lettuce

6 bib lettuce leaves or 10-12
    leaf lettuce leaves
5 cups *fresh, young* shelled
    peas
2 green onions, chopped
2 tbsp butter
1 tbsp chicken stock or water
    (see basic recipes)
½ tsp sugar
½ tsp salt

Line a 2-quart saucepan with the lettuce leaves. Add the peas. Sprinkle on the green onions and add butter, stock, and sugar. Cover and cook gently for 20-30 minutes until the peas are tender. Add the salt. Stir in lightly. Remove from heat and cover again for another 2 minutes. Serve in the cooking dish if possible.

4-5 cups washed, dried, and
crisped dandelion greens
6 slices bacon

Dressing:
1 ½ tsp flour
⅛ tsp dry mustard
½ tsp salt
¼ tsp freshly ground pepper
2 tsp cider vinegar
2 tsp white sugar
¼ cup light sweet cream
½ cup sour cream
2 hard-boiled eggs, finely
chopped

Dandelion Salad with Bacon and Sour Cream Dressing

Break greens into 2″ lengths and place in a salad bowl. Cover. Refrigerate.

Fry the bacon until crisp and drain on paper towel, reserving two tbsp of the bacon fat in the frying pan. Crumble bacon, reserve.

Over low heat, stir the flour, mustard, salt, and pepper into the bacon fat. Add the vinegar, sugar, sweet cream, and sour cream and cook 3-4 minutes or until the sauce is thick and smooth. Pour the hot sauce over the dandelions. Sprinkle on the bacon and egg. Toss well.

one 10″ unbaked, unpricked
pie shell (see basic recipes)

Filling:
2 ½ cups chopped rhubarb
1 cup white sugar
2 tbsp flour
½ tsp mace
2 egg yolks
½ cup light cream or milk
¼ cup melted butter

Meringue:
3 egg whites
½ tsp vinegar
⅛ tsp salt
6 tbsp white sugar
½ tsp vanilla
1 tsp white sugar

Rhubarb Custard Meringue Pie

Filling: Combine the rhubarb with the sugar, flour, and mace. Put the rhubarb into the pie shell. Whisk the egg yolks together with the cream and the melted butter. Pour this custard mixture over the rhubarb.

Place on a rack set in the lower part of the oven at 450 degrees. Bake 10 minutes. Reduce heat to 350 degrees and bake 35-40 minutes or until the custard is set.

Meringue: Beat the egg whites with the vinegar and salt until they are stiff but not dry. Add the 6 tbsp sugar and vanilla. Swirl the meringue onto the pie. Sprinkle with the 1 tsp sugar.

Bake an additional 4 minutes at 425 degrees until delicately browned. Cool and serve as soon as possible.

Classic Double-crust Rhubarb Pie

sufficient pastry for a 2-crust 9″ pie (see basic recipes)

4 cups fresh pink rhubarb, cut into ½″ pieces

1 ½ cups white sugar

¼ cup all-purpose flour

1 tbsp butter

½ tsp freshly grated nutmeg or ½ tsp grated orange rind

1 egg white

2 tsp white sugar

Place the rhubarb in a large bowl. Combine the 1 ½ cups sugar and flour; sprinkle over the rhubarb. Toss to coat the fruit evenly. Line the pie tin with pastry. Do not trim. Arrange the rhubarb in the pie shell, heaping it up slightly in the middle. Dot with butter and sprinkle on the nutmeg.

Moisten the pastry on the rim of the pie plate. Place the top crust over the fruit. Press down all along the rim. Trim the pastry ½″ beyond the outside edge of the pie plate. Dampen the ½″ border around the upper crust. Fold over both crusts towards the pie, press this doubled crust together and flute the edges. Slash 6 steam holes around the centre in the top crust.

Beat the egg white slightly. Brush over the pie. Sprinkle on the 2 tsp sugar.

Bake 15 minutes at 425 degrees, reduce the heat to 350, and bake 35 minutes more or until the crust is golden brown.

Easter Dinner

Crab Puffs

Traditional Crumb Crust Baked Ham
with
Cumberland Sauce or Spiced Red Currant Jelly
or
Glazed Ham with Hot Cider Sauce

Buttered Fiddleheads
or
Asparagus Spears with Hollandaise Sauce

Watercress and Mushroom Salad

Maple Syrup Backwoods Pie
or
Iced Maple Syrup Mousse

Suggested wines:
chilled dry white with hors d'oeuvre
dry red with entrée

The focus of this Easter dinner is the ham. Buying and baking a ham today is simple compared to the work formerly involved in the preparation. Having a supply of ham used to involve home pickling, usually done in the late fall, and smoking, frequently an April event. This process was just the beginning, for the ham had next to be boiled to remove the saltiness. Then it was baked. A favourite way of making the outside crusty was to sprinkle on brandy, sugar, and fine bread crumbs. Ham baked with fruit is a recent innovation.

Although it is fast and simple to buy a precooked ham and just finish it off in the oven, an uncooked ham soaked, boiled, and baked in the traditional way is vastly superior in taste and texture. A fruity cumberland sauce or a spiced red currant jelly accompanies this meat very well.

Easter comes during the maple syrup season, a fact modern cooks often forget. The maple syrup backwoods pie is from the 1915 *Red Roses Cook Book*; it is the ancestor of all runny butter tarts. The iced maple syrup mousse shows up in several cookbooks of the early twentieth century, when ice cream was at a peak of popularity.

Crab Puffs

12 small or 18 tiny cream puffs
  (see basic recipes)

Sauce:
2 tbsp butter
2 tbsp flour
⅔ cup milk
⅔ cup light cream
½ tsp salt
⅛ tsp freshly ground pepper
⅛ tsp freshly grated nutmeg
dash of cayenne pepper

Filling:
2 tbsp butter
2 tbsp finely chopped green
  onions
½ cup finely chopped
  mushrooms
2 cups cooked crabmeat, cut
  into chunks
2 tbsp brandy or dry sherry
1 tbsp very finely chopped
  parsley

Garnish:
watercress

Use either canned crabmeat or frozen crabmeat from Dungeness, King or Queen crabs. If fresh crabs are available, cook as for lobster (see page 64).

Melt the butter for the sauce. Stir in the flour. Cook over medium heat 2-3 minutes. Scald the milk and cream. Stir rapidly into the butter and flour to make a smooth, creamy sauce. Add seasonings. Cook over low heat 4-5 minutes.

Melt the butter for the filling. Add the onions and sauté 2-3 minutes or until transparent. Add the mushrooms. Continue cooking 3-4 more minutes or until the mushrooms are softened. Add the crabmeat. Cook just enough to heat through. Stir in the liquor and parsley. Fold into the sauce. Taste for seasoning. Add more salt if necessary. Heat through.

Cut off the top of a cream puff. Fill with the creamed crab. If serving on a plate, have a little flow over the sides. Put on the top. Garnish with watercress.

If serving as an hors d'oeuvre, make the cream puff paste into 18 puffs and fill each one in the same way, but do not overflow the sauce. Serve on a large tray garnished with watercress.

Traditional Crumb Crust Baked Ham

1 whole ham or butt end, 8-15 lbs, bone in, *uncooked*
2 tbsp brandy
1 cup medium-fine dry bread crumbs
1 tbsp dry mustard
¼ cup firmly packed brown sugar

You may have to order this uncooked ham or search it out. Most supermarkets stock only precooked or partially cooked hams.

Soak ham in cold water to cover (optional, as most hams are not as salty today as home-salted and cured ones used to be).

Place ham on a rack in a large saucepan or preserving kettle. Cover with cold water. Bring to the boil. Remove scum. Reduce heat and simmer 2 hours.

Remove from saucepan, place on a rack in a shallow roasting pan. Bake at 325 degrees 20-30 minutes per pound or according to time suggested on label. Include the simmering time as part of the whole cooking time. Ham is cooked when a meat thermometer registers 160 degrees.

One hour before the end of the cooking time, remove the skin (it will have split by now) and trim the fat neatly. Sprinkle the ham with brandy. Combine the crumbs, mustard, and sugar and press onto the fat. Continue baking. This old-fashioned coating will form a delicious crust on the ham. Ham prepared this way is equally good hot or cold.

Serve with cumberland sauce (see below) or spiced red currant jelly (see preserves recipes at end of book).

Cumberland Sauce

¼ cup finely chopped onions
boiling water
zest, but not the white pith, of 1 orange and 1 lemon
boiling water
juice of the orange
juice of ½ lemon
2 tbsp raisins, chopped
⅓ cup port
⅓ cup red currant jelly made without artificial pectin (see preserves section)
pinch of ground ginger

Parboil the onions 1 minute in boiling water to cover. Drain and reserve.

Cut the orange and lemon zest into fine slivers. Boil rapidly for 5 minutes in water to cover. Drain, rinse in cold water, drain again.

Combine the onions and zest with the rest of the ingredients in a heavy-bottomed saucepan. Bring to the boil and cook over high heat until the jelly has melted. Reduce heat and simmer 5 minutes. Pour into a hot sterilized 8-ounce jar if not to be eaten immediately. If to be used immediately, cool and pour into small serving dish. Yield: about 1 cup.

Glazed Ham with Hot Cider Sauce

1 ham, 8-15 lbs, partially cooked or precooked
1 lemon
1 cup brown sugar, firmly packed
1 tsp ground cloves
1 tsp ground cinnamon
2 ½ cups apple cider
1 cup sultana raisins
½ cup firmly packed brown sugar
1 tsp dry mustard
1 tbsp cornstarch
2 tbsp cold water

Put ham fat side up in a covered roasting pan. Pare the zest but not the white pith off the lemon. Chop zest into slivers. Squeeze juice. Mix 1 cup brown sugar, lemon juice, zest, spices, and cider. Pour over the ham. Cover the ham.

Cook ham 18 minutes per pound at 325 degrees or until a meat thermometer registers 160 degrees. Baste frequently.

Half an hour before end of baking time, add raisins; continue basting.

Combine ½ cup brown sugar and mustard. Press over ham. Return ham to 400-degree oven and roast uncovered until the glaze is set.

Remove the ham to a preheated platter. Carefully skim the fat from the roasting pan. Combine the cornstarch and water. Blend into the sauce in the roasting pan and cook until thickened. Serve sauce in a preheated gravy boat.

Buttered Fiddleheads

1 ½-2 lbs fiddleheads
boiling water
¾ tsp salt
3 tbsp melted butter
2 tsp lemon juice

Wash the fiddleheads thoroughly in several changes of cold water until there are no brown shreds of the papery covering left.

Place in the top of a steamer (or in a large sieve) over boiling water and steam until tender, about 10 to 15 minutes. Sprinkle with salt. Place in a preheated serving dish. Combine the melted butter and lemon juice. Pour over the fiddleheads.

Frozen fiddleheads are now available most of the year in Canada. As with most frozen vegetables, utmost care must be taken not to overcook them. Follow the package instructions carefully. Even with this care, the fiddleheads lose much of their texture and taste after freezing. Nevertheless, this is the only way many Canadians can obtain this spring delicacy.

2-3 lbs fresh, close-tipped
  asparagus
boiling water
1 tsp salt

Asparagus Spears with Hollandaise Sauce

Wash the asparagus thoroughly to remove any sand particles. Break off each stalk as far down as it snaps easily. Do not cut with a knife! The asparagus breaks off naturally where it is no longer tender. Tie the asparagus together loosely and stand it upright in the bottom of a double boiler which has 2-3 inches of boiling water in it.

Invert the top of the double boiler over the asparagus tips. The tougher ends of the stalks will cook in the boiling water while the steam cooks the tips.

When the asparagus is almost ready (7-10 minutes), uncover it and sprinkle with the salt. Recover and cook 2-3 minutes more. Do not let the asparagus get mushy. Drain.

Carefully lift the asparagus onto a warm platter and pour the hollandaise sauce over the middle, leaving the tips and the ends uncovered.

2 egg yolks, lightly beaten
⅓ cup cold butter
1 ½ tbsp lemon juice
½ tsp salt
dash of cayenne pepper

Hollandaise Sauce

Place the egg yolks in a small, heavy-bottomed saucepan. Cut the butter in three pieces, place on the yolks. Add the juice, salt, and cayenne pepper. Place over very low heat and stir with a rubber spatula until the butter is melted. Continue stirring, clearing the bottom of the pan thoroughly, until the sauce is thick and creamy, about 5 minutes. Be sure to keep the heat very low or the sauce will curdle. Remove from heat. Continue stirring for 2 more minutes. Yield: 1 cup.

There are many other ways of making hollandaise sauce. One reliable and easy way is in a blender. The absolutely traditional hollandaise is made over gently boiling water. All hollandaise sauces, however, are made from egg yolks, butter, and lemon juice, no matter what the method used to create the emulsification.

Blender Method Hollandaise

3 egg yolks
2 tbsp lemon juice
½ tsp salt
pinch of freshly ground pepper
   or cayenne
½ cup butter

Place the egg yolks, lemon juice, salt and pepper in the container of the blender. Heat the butter in a small saucepan with a pouring spout until the butter foams up but before it browns.

Cover the blender container and blend the egg yolk mixture at high speed for 3 seconds. Remove the lid (many blenders have smaller inner lids and in this case remove only the inner lid). Continue blending at top speed, and pour the butter into the egg yolk mixture in a steady slow stream. This should take ½ to ¾ of a minute. Stop the blender, taste, blend in more salt and pepper if desired. Yield: about ¾ cup.

Watercress and Mushroom Salad

1 ½ cups very thinly sliced
   mushrooms
1 tbsp finely chopped parsley
1 tbsp finely chopped chives
5 tbsp oil
1 tbsp lemon juice
½ tsp dry mustard
¼ tsp freshly ground pepper
½ tsp salt
4 cups loosely packed
   watercress, leaves and fine
   stems only (1-2 bunches,
   depending on size)

Combine the mushroom slices, parsley, and chives in a small bowl. Blend together the oil, lemon juice, mustard, pepper, and salt and add to the mushrooms. Toss well together. Cover and refrigerate for 15 minutes.

Put the watercress in a large salad bowl, add the mushrooms and dressing, and toss to coat all the leaves. Serve immediately.

Maple Syrup Backwoods Pie

one 10″ unpricked, unbaked
   pie shell (see basic recipes)
2 tbsp butter
1 cup firmly packed brown
   sugar
3 egg yolks
½ cup milk
1 cup pure maple syrup
¼ tsp freshly grated nutmeg
3 egg whites
whipped cream (see basic
   recipes)

Cream together the butter and sugar. Add the egg yolks and beat well. Stir in the milk, maple syrup, and nutmeg.

Beat the egg whites until they are stiff but not dry. Fold the egg whites into the syrup mixture.

Pour into the pie shell. Bake at 450 degrees for 10 minutes. Reduce heat to 350 degrees and bake 30-35 minutes more or until the crust is golden brown and the filling is set.

Serve with whipped cream.

1 cup pure maple syrup
4 eggs, separated
½ tsp vanilla
1 ¼ cups heavy cream
½ cup toasted slivered almonds
   (see basic recipes)

Iced Maple Syrup Mousse

Place the syrup and the egg yolks in the top of a double boiler over boiling water. Beat well together and cook until the syrup thickens, or to 165 degrees on a candy thermometer. Cool. Add the vanilla. Whip the cream until stiff, and mix gently into the syrup. Beat the egg whites until stiff but not dry. Fold into the syrup and cream.

    Pour into a 6-cup mould or container and freeze. To unmould, dip in hot water and turn out on a plate, or scoop into tall glasses. Sprinkle with toasted almond slivers.

Salmon Buffet

Chilled Watercress Soup

Poached Salmon
Asparagus Spears
Green Mayonnaise
Stone-ground Brown Bread

Marinated Cucumber and Onion Rings

Choice of:
Classic Strawberry Shortcake
Meringue Shells
with
Homemade Vanilla Ice Cream and Sliced Strawberries
Strawberry Water Ice

Suggested wine:
chilled Riesling

This light buffet dinner features chilled poached salmon. Of the varieties of salmon available in the spring, the true Atlantic salmon and the British Columbia red spring salmon (weighing about 5-7 pounds) are ideal for a buffet dinner.

Thin slices of stone-ground brown bread go very well with this dish.

I am giving a choice of three desserts, all based on fresh strawberries, including the classic version of strawberry shortcake made with a tea biscuit base. This perennial favourite of strawberry socials is surely one of the great desserts of all time. Wild strawberries, if they can be found at the end of June, will noticeably improve all these desserts.

For the stone-ground brown bread, see the basic recipes section at the end of the book.

3 tbsp butter
1 cup chopped onions (2 medium)
3 cups sliced leeks (2-3 leeks, whites only)
½ cup chopped celery (1 stalk)
2 cups sliced peeled potatoes
3 ½ cups chicken stock (see basic recipes)
1 tsp salt
¼ tsp freshly ground pepper
2 cups chopped watercress, leaves and fine stems only (1-2 bunches, depending on size)
½ cup heavy cream
½ cup light cream (can be increased if a lighter soup is desired)
½ cup chopped watercress leaves
⅔ cup light cream

Chilled Watercress Soup

Melt the butter over medium heat in a large, heavy-bottomed saucepan. Add the onions, leeks, and celery. Stir to coat evenly with butter. Reduce heat to low, cover, and cook 15 minutes.

Add potatoes, stock, salt, pepper, and watercress leaves and fine stems. Simmer covered for 15-20 minutes or until the vegetables are tender.

Pass through a sieve or blend until smooth. Return to a clean saucepan. Add the ½ cup heavy and the ½ cup light cream.

Chill soup. Taste. Add extra salt if desired; cold foods usually require more salt than hot foods. At serving time, stir in watercress leaves and the extra ⅔ cup light cream.

Poached Salmon

1 whole fresh salmon or a
  centre-cut piece, 4-8 lbs
water
1 large onion, chopped
2 carrots, chopped
½ celery stalk, chopped
8 sprigs parsley
1 tsp dill seed or 1 small bunch
  of fresh dill
1 bay leaf
2 whole cloves
1 tbsp coarse salt
½ tsp whole peppercorns
juice of 1 large lemon
1 cup white wine

Garnish:
leaf lettuce
asparagus spears (see page 29)
lemon slices
parsley

Wipe fish and place it in a poacher or saucepan large enough to hold it comfortably. Add enough water to cover. Remove fish. Add the rest of the ingredients to the water. Bring to the boil. Reduce heat. Simmer 20 minutes.

Add the salmon to the liquid. For easy handling, wrap fish in a piece of rinsed cheesecloth large enough to come out over the sides or ends of the poacher. This provides handles for removing the fish once it is cooked. Bring the liquid back to the boil. Boil 2 minutes exactly. Remove from heat. Cover with a tight-fitting lid. Leave to cool completely in the cooking liquid (a large fish can take up to 5 hours).

Drain. Place on an oval serving platter. Chill. If desired, remove the skin of the fish. Surround the fish with curly leaf lettuce and asparagus, parsley, and lemon slices. Serve with green mayonnaise.

It is important to leave enough time for this method of cooking. Begin in the morning for an evening buffet. Length of chilling time may be long, but the reliability and ease of the cooking more than compensate.

To prepare asparagus, follow the recipe on page 29. After cooking, drain and chill.

Green Mayonnaise

1 cup homemade mayonnaise
  (see basic recipes)
2 tbsp finely chopped chives
2 tbsp finely chopped fresh dill
2 tbsp finely chopped
  watercress leaves
2 tbsp finely chopped parsley

Combine all ingredients. Cover and chill for at least 2 hours for the flavour to mature.

Marinated Cucumber and Onion Rings

one 8" fresh cucumber
½ Spanish onion or 1 medium
  red onion or mild cooking
  onion
1 tsp salt
2 tbsp cider vinegar
2 tbsp white sugar
½ tsp freshly ground pepper
½ cup sour cream
1 tbsp finely chopped chives

Rasp the skin of the cucumber with a fork. Slice the cucumber and onion very thin. Sprinkle with salt, cover, and refrigerate for 1 hour. Drain.

Add vinegar, sugar, and pepper. Stir and return covered to the refrigerator. Just before serving, add sour cream and chives and toss.

Shortcake:
2 ½ cups sifted all-purpose
  flour
3 tbsp white sugar
4 tsp baking powder
½ tsp salt
6 tbsp butter
¾-1 cup light cream
2 tbsp soft butter

Other ingredients:
2 cups sliced strawberries
2 tbsp white sugar
½ pint heavy cream
1 tsp white sugar
¼ tsp vanilla
1 cup perfect berries

Classic Strawberry Shortcake

Sift the dry ingredients for the shortcake together into a large bowl. Cut the butter into the dry ingredients with a pastry blender.

Stir the cream in with a fork, pressing the mixture together lightly to form a ball. The amount of cream varies; use only enough to form the ball. Otherwise the dough will be too sticky. Turn the dough onto a lightly-floured board and knead for 1 minute.

Divide the dough in half and roll into 2 equal circles about ½" thick. Place one layer on a lightly-floured baking sheet. Spread with soft butter. Place the other layer on top.

Bake at 425 degrees for 20-25 minutes. Remove from the oven and cool on a rack.

Combine the sliced strawberries with the 2 tbsp sugar. Stir. Let stand 20-30 minutes. While the cake is still very slightly warm, separate the two layers. Trim the edges and place the bottom layer on a doily on a large glass plate. Cover this layer lavishly with the sugared sliced berries. Cover with the second layer.

Whip the cream and add the 1 tsp sugar and the vanilla. Spread the whipped cream over the top and sides of the shortcake. Decorate with the perfect berries. Serve immediately.

4 egg whites at room
  temperature
¼ tsp cream of tartar
1 cup white sugar
¼ tsp salt
¼ tsp almond extract
1 quart strawberries
⅓ cup white sugar
1 tbsp brandy

Meringue Shells with Homemade Vanilla Ice Cream and Sliced Strawberries

Beat the egg whites till foamy. Sprinkle on the cream of tartar and beat until the egg whites stand up in peaks. Continue to beat gradually adding the 1 cup sugar. Stir in the salt and almond extract. Place the meringue into a piping bag and pipe twelve 3" meringue shells formed into nest-like shapes onto a baking sheet lined with a layer of heavy brown paper, or form the 12 shells with a spoon. For crisp white meringues, bake the meringues at the lowest oven setting, 150 degrees, overnight, leaving the door of the oven open as for broiling. In the morning, peel off the paper.

Store the meringues in an airtight container.

To serve, wash, hull, and slice the strawberries and sprinkle the sugar and brandy on them. Cover and leave 1 hour. Stir gently. Place a generous scoop of vanilla ice cream in each meringue and spoon berries lavishly over the top.

1 ½ cups milk
4 egg yolks
¾ cup white sugar
pinch of salt
1 ½ tsp vanilla
2 ½ cups heavy cream

Vanilla Ice Cream

Scald the milk in the top of a double boiler over direct heat until little bubbles form around the edge of the pan.

Beat together the egg yolks, sugar, and salt.

Add 1 cup of the hot milk to the yolks. Blend in well and return to the rest of the hot milk in the top of the double boiler. Place this over simmering water in the bottom of the double boiler and, stirring constantly, cook until the custard thickens enough to coat a spoon, 5-10 minutes or 165 degrees on a thermometer. Add the vanilla. Cool. Stir several times during the cooling period. Cooling can be done over a bowl of ice cubes and water.

Combine the custard with the heavy cream.

Pour into the can of the churn freezer. Cover. Surround the can with crushed ice and salt (street salt is excellent) in the proportion of 3 parts ice to 1 part salt. Pack down firmly. The ice and salt should come to within 1″ of the top of the can. Have more crushed ice and salt ready for later when the first ice settles.

Turn the crank slowly at first, and then when turning becomes more difficult, turn more quickly. Maintain the level of ice and salt throughout. When the mixture is very difficult to turn, after about 12-15 minutes, remove the can. Wipe very carefully to remove any salt. Take out the dasher which is the blade which churns the ice cream. Pack down the ice cream with a spoon. Let the ice cream mature 1-2 hours in the freezer for maximum flavour and smooth texture.

1 cup white sugar
1 cup water
1 ½ cups fresh crushed
    strawberries (about 1 pint)
juice of ½ lemon
juice of ½ orange
pinch of salt

Strawberry Water Ice

Combine sugar and water in a saucepan. Bring this syrup to the boil. Boil 6 minutes. Cool slightly.

Mix together the crushed berries, lemon and orange juice, salt, and syrup.

Pour the mixture into two cake pans or shallow freezing trays and freeze 1-1 ½ hours or until it is mushy.

Transfer the frozen mixture to a chilled mixing bowl. Beat well with an electric beater until the mixture takes on a creamy smooth appearance.

Spoon into a container with a tight fitting lid and refreeze.

This water ice is best eaten before it is frozen too hard.

Spring Tea

Hot Cheese Rolls

Sandwich Trays of Stone-ground Brown Bread
and
Traditional Potato Bread
with
Watercress and Nasturtium Flowers
Smoked Sturgeon
Smoked Beef
Classic Chicken Salad
Rolled Asparagus

Lemon Loaf and Apricot Nut Loaf
Fresh Unhulled Strawberries
Vanilla Cream Cake

Tea   Raspberry Vinegar   Royal Strawberry Acid

The perfect spring tea is held on a fresh afternoon in a garden of blooming lilac and lily of the valley. There should be a selection of light, crisp sandwiches with such fillings as watercress, smoked beef, and chicken salad.

Watercress is easily one of the most elegant of the early spring vegetables. Suzanna Moodie, on a trip to Niagara Falls in 1853, described it growing on the hill under which Queenston is built:

> Numerous springs wind like silvery threads along the face of the steep bank above; and wherever the waters find a flat ledge in their downward course, water-cresses of the finest quality grow in abundance, the sparkling water gurgling among their juicy leaves, and washing them to emerald brightness. Large portions of the cliff are literally covered with them. It was no small matter of surprise to me when told that the inhabitants made no use of this delicious plant, but laugh at the eagerness with which strangers seek it out. (*Life in the Clearings*)

A tea party must always have a special cake. Recipes for cream cake like the vanilla cream cake recipe included here appeared frequently in the turn-of-the-century personal cookery books.

For the raspberry vinegar and the royal strawberry acid please refer to the preserves section.

2 cups sifted all-purpose flour
1 tsp cream of tartar
½ tsp soda
½ tsp salt
1-1 ¼ cups heavy cream
1 cup grated old cheddar
cheese

Hot Cheese Rolls

Sift the flour, cream of tartar, soda, and salt into a large mixing bowl. With a fork, gradually stir in the cream, up to 1 ¼ cups if necessary in order to incorporate all the dry ingredients. Turn out onto a lightly floured board. Roll out into a rectangular shape about ⅜" thick. Spread with the grated cheese. Roll up as for a jelly roll. Moisten the long edge with water and press to seal. Cut into slices about ⅝" thick. Place flat on an ungreased, lightly floured baking sheet. Bake at 400 degrees until light brown, 10 to 12 minutes. Remove from the sheet immediately. Serve hot. Yield: about 2 ½ dozen.

1 loaf stone-ground brown
bread (see basic recipes)
1 ½ loaves traditional potato
bread
sweet butter
¼ lb thinly sliced smoked
sturgeon
¼ lb thinly sliced smoked beef
lemon slices
1 bunch watercress
8-12 nasturtium flowers (petals
only)
chicken salad (see below)
16 cooked slender asparagus
spears (see Easter dinner
menu)
mayonnaise (see basic recipes)
2 tbsp finely chopped parsley
toothpicks

Sandwich Trays

For open-faced smoked sturgeon and smoked beef sandwiches, cut 8 thin slices of the stone-ground brown bread. Trim the crusts, butter evenly with sweet butter, cut into thirds, and lay thin slices of sturgeon on 12 of these fingers and beef on the other 12. Garnish each open-faced sturgeon sandwich with a very thin slice of lemon.

Cut 16 thin slices of the brown bread for the watercress and nasturtium flower sandwiches. Trim and butter evenly with sweet butter. Lay watercress on 4 slices and nasturtium flowers on 4. Cover with the remaining buttered slices and cut into quarters.

Prepare the chicken salad in advance. Slice 1 loaf of the potato bread into 24 thin slices. Trim the crusts, butter, and spread 12 slices evenly with chicken salad. Cover with the other 12 buttered bread slices and quarter.

For the asparagus rolls, cut 8 thin slices of the potato bread, trim the crusts, spread with mayonnaise, and sprinkle with parsley. Divide in half diagonally. Lay a spear along the long side, extending the asparagus about ¼" over each end. Trim the stalk if necessary. Roll up towards the wide-angled peak and secure with a toothpick.

Garnish a large tray with watercress, nasturtium flowers and leaves, and parsley. Arrange the sandwiches, organizing the open-faced fingers, the quartered sandwiches, and the rolls attractively.

Serve with bowls of the best pickles, such as dilled bean sticks, Indian pickles, pickled carrots, and icicle pickles (see preserves recipes at end of book).

1 package active dry yeast (2 tsp)
1 tsp sugar
½ cup lukewarm unsalted potato water
1 cup warm unsalted very well mashed potatoes
¼ cup butter
3 tbsp sugar
1 ½ tsp salt
¾ cup scalded milk
1 egg, well beaten
4-4 ½ cups sifted all-purpose flour

Traditional Potato Bread

Dissolve the yeast and the 1 tsp sugar in potato water. Let stand 10 minutes.

Combine mashed potatoes, butter, sugar, salt, and scalded milk in a large mixing bowl. Stir well. Set aside until lukewarm.

Add the yeast mixture and egg to the mashed potato mixture. Stir in 2 cups of flour. Turn out onto a well floured board and knead in enough of the rest of the flour to make a soft dough. Knead until the dough is smooth and elastic, about 8 minutes.

Place the dough in a well-greased bowl, turning it over to grease on all sides. Cover with a damp cloth. Let rise 1 to 1 ½ hours or until almost double in bulk.

Punch down to original size, form into 2 loaves, and place in 2 well-greased 9" x 4" loaf tins. Cover lightly and let rise till double in bulk, about 1 hour.

Uncover and bake at 400 degrees for 30-40 minutes or until the bread sounds hollow when tapped. Remove from the pans immediately and cool on a rack.

Cooked chicken:
one 4-5 lb stewing chicken
1 tbsp salt
10 peppercorns
1 bay leaf
4 stalks parsley
½ tsp dried crushed thyme (1 tsp fresh, chopped)
1 large onion, quartered
1 large carrot, roughly chopped
1 celery stalk, roughly chopped
boiling water

Chicken salad:
2 ½ cups finely chopped cooked chicken (white meat is preferable)
1 tbsp very finely chopped tops of green onions or chives
¼ cup finely chopped tender celery
¼ cup finely chopped toasted almonds (see basic recipes)
½ tsp salt
¼ tsp freshly ground pepper
2 tsp lemon juice
¾-1 cup mayonnaise (see basic recipes)

Classic Chicken Salad

Place the chicken, seasonings, and vegetables in a large stock pot. Pour on enough boiling water to cover. Bring to the boil. Remove scum carefully, reduce heat, cover and simmer 3-4 hours or until the chicken is very tender.

Lift the chicken from the pot, and cool. Remove the skin, and take the meat off the bones. Prepare the 2½ cups of finely chopped chicken. It is preferable to use white meat only.

Combine all the ingredients for the chicken salad except mayonnaise. Toss well to distribute seasoning.

Bind with mayonnaise to desired consistency. Chill. Taste. Add more salt if desired.

(One stewing chicken will yield considerably more meat than is required for the sandwiches. Using cut-up chicken portions is an alternative, but the meat will not be as tasty. Another alternative is to use the rest of the meat for chicken salad which can be served on another occasion. For chicken salad served on lettuce, double the quantities in the recipe for chicken salad given here, chop the chicken and celery larger, and sliver the almonds. You may also increase the quantity of celery. Decorate with slices of hard-boiled egg and capers to taste.)

2 cups sifted all-purpose flour
4 tsp baking powder
¾ tsp salt
⅔ cup white sugar
¾ cup finely chopped dried apricots, uncooked
1 cup chopped walnuts
1 egg, lightly beaten
1 cup milk
3 tbsp melted butter, cooled

Apricot Nut Loaf

Sift together the flour, baking powder, salt, and sugar. Add the apricots and walnuts.

Combine the egg, milk, and melted butter. Add to the dry ingredients, mixing only until the ingredients are blended.

Pour into a greased 9″ x 4″ loaf tin. Bake at 375 degrees for 1 hour or until a skewer inserted in the centre comes out clean.

Cool 10 minutes in the pan, turn out onto a rack. Cool, wrap, and store 1 day before slicing.

Lemon Loaf

¼ cup butter
¾ cup white sugar
2 eggs
grated rind of 2 lemons
2 cups sifted all-purpose flour
4 tsp baking powder
½ tsp salt
⅞ cup milk

Topping:
2 tbsp white sugar
3 tbsp lemon juice

Cream the butter till light and fluffy. Add the ¾ cup sugar and beat well. Add the eggs, one at a time, beating after each addition. Stir in the lemon rind.

Sift together the flour, baking powder, and salt. Add in 3 parts alternately with the milk in 2 parts to the creamed mixture. Start and finish with the dry ingredients.

Grease a 9″ x 4″ loaf tin. Line the bottom with a strip of waxed paper. Grease the paper.

Pour batter into the loaf tin and bake at 350 degrees for 55 minutes.

Combine the 2 tbsp sugar and lemon juice. Spread over the top of the loaf and return it to the oven for 5 more minutes.

Remove from the oven and let cool 10 minutes. Remove from the tin. Cool on a rack. Wrap and store 1 day before eating.

Slice and spread with *sweet* butter.

Vanilla Cream Cake

½ cup butter
1 ½ cups white sugar
3 eggs, separated
1 tsp vanilla
2 ½ cups sifted cake flour
1 tbsp baking powder
½ tsp salt
1 cup milk
whipped cream (see basic recipes)

Grease three 8″ or two 9″ cake tins. Line the bottoms with waxed paper. Grease the paper.

Cream the butter till light and fluffy. Gradually beat in the sugar. Add the egg yolks one at a time, beating well after each one. Stir in the vanilla.

Sift together the flour, baking powder, and salt. Add in three parts alternately with the milk in two parts to the creamed mixture. Begin and end with the dry ingredients.

Beat the egg whites till stiff but not dry. Fold into the cake batter.

Bake at 350 degrees about 25-30 minutes for three 8″ layers or 30-35 minutes for two 9″ layers or until a skewer inserted in centre comes out clean. The centre of the cake should spring back when lightly touched.

Cool 10 minutes. Turn out onto a rack. Pull off the waxed paper and let cool.

To serve, place bottom layer on a cake stand, cover with vanilla custard cream filling (see below), add top layer and ice with sweetened whipped cream (see basic recipes). Serve immediately.

¼ cup white sugar
2 tbsp flour
⅛ tsp salt
¾ cup milk
2 egg yolks, well beaten
1 tbsp butter
1 tsp vanilla

Vanilla Custard Cream Filling

Combine sugar, flour and salt. Scald milk in the top of a double boiler placed over direct heat. Gradually add the hot milk to the dry ingredients, mixing thoroughly. Return to the top of the double boiler and cook over boiling water until thickened, stirring constantly. Cover and cook 10 minutes more.

Mix about ¼ cup of the hot custard with the egg yolks and then stir back into the rest of the custard in the double boiler. Blend well. Cook 2 minutes more. Remove from the heat. Add butter and vanilla. Cool.

Leisurely Spring Breakfast

Rhubarb Compote
or
Fresh Pineapple

Apple Cider Baked Bacon
Scrambled Eggs

Hot Cross Buns   Toast

Assortment of:
Platter Strawberry Jam
Pineapple-Rhubard Conserve
Clover Honey
Buckwheat Honey
Seville Orange Marmalade

Coffee   Tea

Hot cross buns are traditional English Easter sweet buns filled with currants and glazed with a sweet icing, dating from the eighteenth century.

Platter jam is an unusual jam recipe handed down from original settlers in Ontario's St. Thomas area. The berries and sugar are boiled together briefly and then poured out onto a platter. The next day the jam is poured into sterilized jars. Platter jam keeps its fresh berry flavour and has a pleasantly runny consistency.

Nothing could be more appropriate for the main dish of a spring breakfast than a piece of back bacon cooked in sweet cider and glazed with honey. The real smokey back bacon is justly famous as "Canadian bacon."

For the jam, conserve and marmalade recipes, see the preserves section at the end of the book.

Rhubarb Compote

6 cups rhubarb, cut into 1"
  pieces
1 cup white sugar (1 ⅓ cups if
  sweeter fruit is desired)
1 cup water
½" piece of cinnamon stick

Combine the sugar, water, and cinnamon stick in the top of a double boiler over direct heat. Bring to the boil. Place over boiling water and add the rhubarb. Spoon some of the syrup over the fruit, cover, and cook over moderately boiling water 15 minutes. Turn the heat off and let the rhubarb cool in the top of the double boiler over the hot water. Do not stir at all. If the rhubarb is cooked this way, the fruit holds its shape and none of the delicate pink colour is lost.

Remove the cinnamon stick and chill. Serve in a clear glass bowl.

Fresh Pineapple

1 ripe fresh pineapple
½ cup brown sugar
1 cup sour cream

Peel, core, and dice the pineapple. Serve in a large bowl. Pass the brown sugar and sour cream for individual servings.

Apple Cider Baked Bacon

2 lbs back bacon in one piece
water to cover
½ cup apple cider
⅛ tsp ground cloves

and either:
4 tbsp brown sugar
¼ tsp dry mustard
1 tbsp cornstarch
1 tsp vinegar

or:
2 tbsp honey

Simmer back bacon in water for one hour. Drain and place in an open, heatproof dish. Pour on cider. Sprinkle with cloves.

Bake at 325 degrees for 45 minutes, basting 4-5 times. To finish off, use either of the following methods. (A) Combine brown sugar, mustard, cornstarch, and vinegar. Spread on bacon. Bake 15 minutes more. Grill if necessary to form crust. (B) Spread with honey instead of the above mixture and bake 15 minutes, grilling if necessary.

Remove from the dish, cut neatly into ¼" slices, and arrange around the scrambled eggs on a preheated platter.

Scrambled Eggs

12 large eggs
¾ tsp salt
¼ tsp freshly grated pepper
¼ cup butter
⅓ cup heavy cream

Beat the eggs lightly with the salt and pepper. Melt the butter in the top of a double boiler. Add the eggs, cook gently, stirring and scraping up from the bottom as the eggs thicken. Just before the eggs set, stir in the cream. Serve immediately on a preheated platter.

1 package active dry yeast (2 tsp)
1 tsp white sugar
¼ cup warm water
½ cup butter
½ cup white sugar
1 cup minus 1 tbsp milk, scalded
1 egg, well beaten
4 cups all-purpose flour
¼ tsp salt
1 ¼ tsp ground cinnamon
½ tsp freshly grated nutmeg
½ tsp ground cardamom
½ tsp ground cloves
½ tsp ground allspice
1 cup currants or raisins
⅓ cup candied mixed peel
1 egg white
2 drops vanilla
icing sugar

Hot Cross Buns

Dissolve the yeast and 1 tsp sugar in the water. Let stand 10 minutes.

Combine the butter and ½ cup sugar. Add the scalded milk. Stir to dissolve the sugar and to melt the butter. Cool to lukewarm.

Add the yeast mixture and the egg to the milk mixture.

Sift together the flour, salt, and spices. Reserve 2 tbsp to dredge the currants and peel. Beat the rest into the batter mixture, first using an electric mixer and then, when that becomes too difficult, a wooden spoon. Turn the dough out onto a floured board. Knead in the raisins and mixed peel and continue kneading for about 10 minutes or until the dough is smooth and elastic. Form the dough into a ball; place in a greased bowl, turning to grease all sides. Cover with a damp cloth and set in a warm place to rise until double in bulk, about 1 hour.

Punch the dough down to original size. Turn out onto a lightly floured board.

Shape the dough into 18 buns and place 2″ apart on a greased baking sheet. Cover loosely and let rise in a warm place till double in bulk, about 1 hour.

Cut a shallow cross on the top of each bun.

Beat the egg white till frothy. Brush lightly on each bun. Keep the rest of the egg white.

Bake at 375 degrees for 10 minutes, reduce heat to 350 degrees and bake for 10 to 15 minutes longer or until the buns are browned and sound hollow when tapped.

Combine the rest of the egg white with the vanilla and enough icing sugar to thicken. Frost the crosses of the hot buns with this icing. Yield: 18 buns.

24th of May Picnic

Devilled Eggs

Pan-fried Minted Brook Trout
Cheese Herb Bread with Sweet Butter

Spring Salad

Fullarton May Cakes with Fudge Icing
or
Classic Butter Tarts

Suggested wine:
chilled dry white (or cold lager beer)

The 24th of May may not be on the 24th of May any longer, since the actual date of the holiday was changed in 1952 to the first Monday in May preceding May 25th. It was first declared a holiday in 1845 by the combined Legislatures of Canada East and Canada West to celebrate Queen Victoria's birthday. Ever since, it has been the day for patriotic displays, flag flying, military parades, band concerts, and fireworks. The Victoria Day Holiday, as it is officially known, is the weekend for all those rites of spring Canadian style: outings to the country or the cottage, the first barefoot paddle in the creeks or the lake, planting the garden, or—best of all—picnics.

6 large eggs
water
2 tsp mayonnaise (see basic
   recipes)
2 tsp boiled dressing (see basic
   recipes)
2 tsp heavy cream
⅓ tsp salt
⅛ tsp dry mustard
⅛ tsp freshly ground pepper
2 tsp finely chopped green
   onions or chives
2 tsp finely chopped parsley

Devilled Eggs

Place the eggs in one layer in a saucepan. Cover with cold water. Put on a close fitting lid. Bring rapidly to the boil. Immediately turn off the heat and leave for 20 minutes. Drain and immediately cool in cold running water. Peel. Slice lengthwise. Remove the yolks.

Mash the yolks thoroughly with a fork. Add the remaining ingredients and blend till smooth. Taste, add more salt if desired. Pipe or spoon into egg whites. Cover and refrigerate for an hour for the flavour to mature. When serving, you may garnish each egg with parsley sprigs, thin slices of pimento, or sliced olives.

For variety of flavour, add ¼ tsp dried crushed oregano, chili powder, or curry powder to the yolk mixture.

6 trout, about ½ lb each
¼ cup flour
1 ½ tsp salt
¾ tsp freshly ground pepper
½ cup butter, clarified
¾ cup heavy cream
3 tbsp finely chopped chives
1 tsp finely chopped fresh mint
fresh mint sprigs

Pan-fried Minted Brook Trout

Wash and wipe the trout, making sure that the cavities are well cleaned.

Combine the flour, salt, and pepper in a bag. Gently shake each trout in the seasoned flour. Lay on a piece of waxed paper.

To clarify butter, melt the ½ cup butter over low heat. Skim off the clear fat and leave the creamy mass in the pan. Frying with only clear fat of the butter means that the butter will not burn. If, however, you like a nutty flavour, use 6 tbsp unclarified butter and be careful not to heat the pan too hot.

Pour the clarified butter into a frying pan (or pans) large enough to accommodate the trout easily. Fry gently about 5 minutes on each side or until the eyes cloud over, the flesh firms up, and the skin is nicely browned. Remove from the pan. Place on a preheated serving platter. Pour the cream into the pan. Stir to scrape up all the particles from the pan. Heat through, add the chives and mint, and pour some over each fish. Decorate the platter with sprigs of fresh mint.

2 packages active dry yeast (4 tsp)
2 cups lukewarm water
2 tbsp white sugar
2 tsp salt
2 tbsp soft butter
½ cup plus 2 tbsp finely grated old cheddar cheese
1 ½ tbsp dried crushed marjoram or 2 tbsp chopped fresh marjoram
4 ½ cups sifted all-purpose flour

Cheese Herb Bread

Sprinkle the yeast over the water in a large mixing bowl. Let stand 10 minutes, then stir to dissolve.

Add the sugar, salt, butter, ½ cup of cheese, marjoram, and 3 cups of the flour. Beat with an electric mixer or by hand until very smooth.

Beat in the rest of the flour by hand. This bread is not kneaded. Cover the bowl with waxed paper and a towel. Let rise in a warm place, 45-60 minutes or until light and bubbly and more than double in bulk.

Stir down the batter, beat vigorously 1 minute. Turn into 2 well greased 9″ x 4″ loaf pans. Sprinkle with the remaining 2 tbsp of cheese. Cover lightly and let rise 30 minutes.

Bake at 375 degrees for 30 minutes or until nicely browned and sounding hollow when tapped. Turn out immediately and cool on a rack.

Yield: 2 medium loaves. This bread is also nice baked in 2 greased 1-quart soufflé dishes.

Slice and spread with sweet butter.

6-8 cups spring greens, for example, torn leaf lettuce, garden cress, tender dandelion shoots, nasturtium greens, watercress
4 radishes, sliced
2 tbsp finely chopped chives or wild leeks

Dressing:
½ cup heavy cream
2 tbsp cider vinegar
1 tsp white sugar
½ tsp salt
¼ tsp freshly ground pepper
⅛ tsp dry mustard

Spring Salad

Place salad ingredients in a large bowl.

Combine ingredients for dressing. Just before serving, pour over the greens and toss.

Fullarton May Cakes

¼ cup butter
½ cup firmly packed brown
   sugar
2 eggs
2 tbsp molasses
1 ½ cups sifted all-purpose
   flour
½ tsp salt
1 tsp ground cinnamon
½ tsp ground cloves
½ tsp freshly grated nutmeg
1 tsp soda
½ cup buttermilk or sour milk
½ cup raisins
½ cup chopped nuts

Cream butter until light and fluffy. Add the sugar gradually, beating well. Beat in the eggs, one at a time. Stir in the molasses.

Sift together flour, salt, and spices. Dissolve the soda in the buttermilk. Use 2 tbsp of the sifted ingredients to dredge the raisins and nuts.

Add the dry ingredients in 3 parts alternating with the buttermilk in 2 parts to the creamed mixture. Begin and end with dry ingredients. Stir in the dredged raisins and nuts. Spoon into well-greased muffin tins.

Bake at 375 degrees for 20-25 minutes or until the cakes leave the sides of the tins. Remove from tins and cool on a rack. Ice with fudge icing (see below). Yield: 12 large cupcakes.

Fudge Icing for May Cakes

1 cup light cream
3 cups firmly packed brown
   sugar
⅛ tsp salt
3 tbsp butter
1 tsp vanilla

Place cream and sugar and salt in a heavy-bottomed saucepan. Stir over low heat until the sugar dissolves. Using a candy thermometer, boil without stirring to soft-ball stage (238 degrees). Remove from the heat. Cool to lukewarm, without stirring. Add the butter and vanilla. Beat until thick and creamy. Spread quickly over the May cakes before the icing hardens.

Classic Butter Tarts

sufficient pastry for 1 dozen
   unbaked and unpricked tart
   shells (see basic recipes)
½ cup currants or raisins
water
¼ cup soft butter
½ cup firmly packed brown
   sugar
2 eggs, lightly beaten
1 cup corn syrup
1 tsp vanilla

Place currants or raisins in a sieve and set over simmering water for 5 minutes to plump up. Remove and drain on a paper towel.

Blend together the butter and brown sugar. Stir in the eggs, corn syrup, and vanilla. Tarts will be runnier and less likely to bubble over if stirring is kept to a minimum. Add the raisins or currants.

Fill the tart shells ⅔ full.

Bake at 375 degrees for 15-20 minutes or until the pastry is golden. Remove from the tins carefully and cool on a rack.

Summer

Summer is the shortest but the most abundant season in Canada. Compressed into July and August is a steady succession of prime fruits and vegetables. It is difficult to do justice to each fruit in turn—cherries, currants, gooseberries, raspberries, peaches, apricots, early transparent apples, plums, and pears. Luscious vegetables also follow one after the other and overlap considerably—lettuce, peas, radishes, beans, spinach, beets, carrots, tomatoes, summer squash, green peppers, corn, cucumbers, onions, and potatoes. By staggering the planting and choosing varieties that ripen over different lengths of time, a gardener can have a steady crop all summer. The quality of Canadian vegetables has long been noteworthy:

> All the vegetables are particularly good and I eat little else. The Asiatics eat no meat in the summer and I dare say they are right and the heat nearly approaches to that in the East. The people here in the summer live chiefly on vegetables and a little salt pork. (Mrs. Simcoe, August 13, 1795)

July and August see the ripening of the best of our wild fruits—chokecherries, raspberries, blueberries, blackberries, elderberries, and may-apples. As more of our countryside disappears under development, fewer and fewer people are able to experience the pleasures of gathering these fruits. Raspberries, blueberries, and blackberries can be eaten raw or made into countless desserts, preserves, and fermented or unfermented drinks. Chokecherries make excellent wine and jelly, and elderberries do triple service in wine, pies, and preserves.

After hockey, the great national sport must be fishing. The lakes of the Laurentian Shield and Northern Canada provide some of the world's finest angling. Because most people still vacation in the summer, fish is an important part of summer eating. Although the pickerel season opens in mid-May, it flourishes into the summer; so does the pike, musky, bass, and perch season. Yellow pickerel has firm, flaky, white flesh, superior to the pike and maskinonge for its reliably fine flavour. Black bass is also an unusually good eating fish, but you almost have to catch it yourself; it is very unlikely that you will find freshwater black bass for sale.

The summer heat combined with a vacation atmosphere encourages us to eat outside. For cooks, this is a pleasant challenge. All sorts of fish, poultry, and meat take on new quality when barbecued. And certain salad and vegetable dishes just naturally taste better at picnics than they ever could in the dining room. The great picnic occasion is July 1st. Dominion Day was fixed as a holiday by Royal Proclamation in 1867 and is still joyously celebrated by post-Centennial Canadians with concerts, parades, strawberry festivals, giant picnics, and fireworks.

One special aspect of summer food is the art of preserving some of it at its peak for the winter months. It is no longer necessary for variety of diet, for economy or certainly for survival to make jams, preserves, pickles, and relishes or to dry fruit, but still there remains an old urge in many Canadians not to waste and to make at least a few jars of jam or pickle for winter.

Summer Barbecue

Fresh Garden Vegetable Platter with Russian Dressing Dip

Grilled Porterhouse Steaks with Lemon and Chive Butter
Corn on the Cob
Oatmeal Bread

Hellfire Salad
or
Summer Herb Tomato Salad

Choice of Summer Fruit Pies:
Raspberry Cream Tart
Schnitz Peach Pie
Open Gooseberry Tart

Suggested wine:
robust red (or beer)

The historical precedent for the modern barbecue was broiling on a gridiron. This iron cooking utensil sat over the coals in a hearth; it was circular in shape with cross bars for the food and had three legs that rested in the coals and a long handle—very like our charcoal barbecue.

The hellfire salad in this menu is popular around Stratford, Ontario, even though delicate Stratford ladies have been known to hesitate over the name. It is a combination of the best fresh vegetables from the garden—tomatoes, onions, cucumbers, and green peppers—plus slivers of hot red pepper, which give it its name.

Fruit pies are probably the favourite desserts of Canada. I'm giving a choice of three delicious ones. The recipe for raspberry cream pie has done a bit of travelling. It first appears in the 1831 *Cook Not Mad* and later shows up word for word in the 1861 *Manual of Cookery*, which the editor describes as "compiled from the best English, French and American works especially adapted to this country."

Russian Dressing:
2 cups homemade mayonnaise
   (see basic recipes)
1 tsp dry or mild prepared
   mustard
1 tsp Worcestershire sauce
¼ cup chili sauce, puréed or
   sieved (see preserves section)
¼ cup very finely chopped
   green onion or chives
1 tsp finely chopped parsley
1 tsp finely chopped capers

Fresh Garden Vegetable Platter with Russian Dressing

Choose a selection of vegetables, some to be cooked to crisp-tender, the majority to be raw and crisp. You will need 2-3 pounds all together. For the cooked vegetables, simmer green or yellow beans, snow peas, or broccoli spears in separate pans of unsalted water 4-5 minutes or until crisp-tender. Drain and chill. Cut raw carrots, zucchini, celery, and unpeeled cucumbers into sticks. Leave radishes, tiny tomatoes, and small white mushrooms whole. Trim green onions. Break up cauliflower into medium-small flowerets and cut green and sweet red pepper into rings or strips. Choose your favourites from among these, keeping in mind a good taste and colour contrast. Chill all the vegetables.

To make the dressing, blend together all the ingredients, and, if possible, leave 2-3 hours to mature the flavour.

Place the dressing in a bowl in the middle of a platter or tray. Arrange the vegetables attractively around the bowl. To eat, dip the vegetables in the dressing.

---

six 1″ porterhouse steaks, well
   hung and trimmed
oil
freshly ground pepper
salt

Grilled Porterhouse Steaks with Lemon and Chive Butter

One hour before grilling time, remove steaks from refrigerator. Smear with oil and grind black pepper on both sides. Snip fat edges of the meat. Let come to room temperature.

Grill 5″ from the coals, turning once during the cooking, 5-6 minutes for rare, 8-9 minutes for medium, and 10-13 minutes for well-done. Salt each side after it is cooked.

Serve with curls of lemon and chive butter.

Lemon and Chive Butter

6 tbsp soft butter
¾ tsp salt
⅓ tsp freshly ground pepper
¾ tsp dry mustard
¼ tsp grated lemon peel
1 tbsp lemon juice
1 ½ tbsp very finely chopped chives
1 tsp very finely chopped parsley

Combine all ingredients. Work well together. Press down. Refrigerate. Place curls of this butter on each steak as it is removed from the grill.

Corn on the Cob

6-12 ears of tender pale yellow corn, preferably straight from the garden
boiling water
soft butter
salt
pepper

Remove the husks and silk from the corn. Drop ears into a large pot of boiling water. Boil 3-5 minutes or until tender. Remove, serve with lots of soft butter, salt, and pepper.

Oatmeal Bread

1 package active dry yeast (2 tsp)
1 tsp brown sugar
¼ cup lukewarm water
1 cup rolled oats (not the instant variety)
¼ cup molasses or maple syrup
1 tsp salt
2 tbsp butter
2 cups boiling water
1 cup whole wheat flour
3-4 cups all-purpose or hard unbleached white flour
1 tsp melted butter

Dissolve the yeast and sugar in the lukewarm water. Let stand 10 minutes in a warm spot.

Place the rolled oats, molasses, salt, and butter in a large mixing bowl. Pour on the boiling water. Stir to dissolve the molasses and melt the butter. Cool to lukewarm.

Combine the rolled oats and yeast mixtures. Using an electric beater, add the whole wheat flour and as much of the all-purpose flour as you can (about 1-2 cups). Turn out the dough onto a liberally floured board and knead in the rest of the all-purpose flour. You know you have added enough when the dough is smooth and no longer sticky. Knead 8-10 minutes in all. Shape into a round ball.

Place the dough in a large greased bowl, turning to grease all sides. Cover the bowl with a damp cloth. Let rise until double in bulk, 1-1 ½ hours, in a warm spot. (A just-warmed oven is ideal.)

Punch down the dough to original size. Form into two oval loaves. Place in two well-greased 9″ x 4″ loaf tins. Cover lightly in a warm place and let rise again until double in bulk, about 1-1 ½ hours.   *continued*

Bake at 375 degrees for 30-40 minutes or until the loaves sound hollow when tapped.

Remove from tins, brush tops with melted butter, cool on a rack.

Hellfire Salad

3 cups peeled and coarsely chopped tomatoes
¾ cup chopped cucumber (leave skin on if tender)
½ cup chopped green pepper
1 tsp very finely slivered hot red pepper
½ cup finely chopped onion
1 tsp chopped fresh basil, summer savory, or marjoram

Dressing:
2 tbsp cider vinegar
1 tbsp brown sugar
½ tsp freshly ground pepper
1 tsp salt

Garnish:
finely chopped parsley

Combine all ingredients, stir to blend flavours. Garnish with parsley to taste.

Summer Herb Tomato Salad

6-8 fine ripe tomatoes
1 small onion

Dressing:
½ cup olive oil
2 tbsp lemon juice
¾ tsp salt
½ tsp freshly ground pepper
½ tsp chopped fresh marjoram
1 tsp chopped fresh basil
2 tbsp finely chopped fresh parsley
1 clove minced garlic

Remove the core from the tomatoes and cut them in vertical slices. Peel and slice the onion and separate into rings. Arrange the tomato slices and onion rings in layers in a shallow bowl.

Combine the ingredients for the dressing and pour over the tomatoes and onions. Cover and refrigerate 15 minutes before serving.

sufficient puff pastry for a
    2-crust 10" pie (see basic
    recipes)
1 egg white
1 tbsp water
4 cups raspberries
¾ cup white sugar
2 tbsp cornstarch
½ cup thick cream
2 egg yolks, lightly beaten

Raspberry Cream Tart

Line pie plate with puff pastry rolled ⅛" thick. Trim the edges and press down with the tines of a fork all around the rim of the pie plate.

Beat the egg white and water together till frothy. Brush the forked rim of the pastry with this egg wash. Chill the pie shell 30 minutes.

Pour the raspberries into the pie shell.

Combine the sugar and cornstarch. Sprinkle over the berries.

Bake at 425 degrees for 20-25 minutes or until the crust is golden brown.

As soon as the pie is in the oven, cut a second circle of pastry the same size as the bottom and place on an ungreased baking sheet. Brush with the egg-white glaze, decorate with pieces of dough cut into leaf shapes, press around the edges with a fork in a similar pattern to the bottom crust. Bake 20 minutes at 425 degrees. It should be puffy and golden. Remove and reserve.

Combine the cream and egg yolks. Pour over the raspberries. Return to oven 10 minutes. Remove, place baked crust over berries and custard and bake an additional 5 minutes until the custard is set.

one deep 9" pie shell
    unpricked and unbaked (see
    basic recipes)
4 cups peeled, sliced peaches
¼ cup heavy cream
½ tsp freshly grated nutmeg
¼ cup firmly packed brown
    sugar
¼ cup white sugar
2 tbsp flour
⅛ tsp salt
2 tbsp butter

Schnitz Peach Pie

Arrange peach slices attractively in pie shell. Pour cream over peaches. Sprinkle on nutmeg.

Combine the brown and white sugar, flour, and salt. Using a pastry blender, cut the butter into the dry ingredients. Sprinkle this mixture over the peaches.

Bake at 425 degrees for 15 minutes. Reduce heat to 350 degrees and cook for 35 minutes more or until the peaches are tender and the crust is golden brown.

one 9" pie plate lined with
    sweet pastry (see below)
4 cups ripe gooseberries
1 cup white sugar
⅛ tsp ground mace
1 egg yolk
¼ cup heavy cream

Open Gooseberry Tart

Top and tail gooseberries. Wash and dry. Place in the lined pie plate. Sprinkle on the sugar and mace. Bake at 350 degrees for 20 minutes.

Beat the egg yolk lightly with the cream and drizzle over the gooseberries. Return to oven, bake 18 minutes more or until the pastry is lightly browned and the berries tender.

Best served when just cooled.

1 cup sifted all-purpose flour
1 egg yolk
1 tbsp white sugar
½ cup soft butter
½ tsp grated lemon rind
1-2 tbsp ice water

Sweet Pastry

Place the flour in a bowl. Make a well in the centre and put the egg yolk, sugar, butter, and lemon rind into the well. Using one hand, work these ingredients together in the centre, then gradually incorporate the flour. Add only as much water as is necessary to form a ball and absorb all the crumbs. Wrap and chill 1 hour.

Summer Lunch

Chilled Consommé with Chives

Fish Salad with Herbed Mayonnaise
Graham Flour Finger Rolls with Sweet Butter

Summer Fruit Bowl with Mint Leaves
Clotted Cream

Iced Russian Tea

Suggested wine:
chilled dry white

The highlight of this summer lunch is the fish salad. The recipe
for it in the 1861 *Manual of Cookery* indicates using lobster
alone, but suggests that crabs or other fish would be suitable. A
combination of whitefish with pink and red shellfish gives a nice
colour and texture. The *Manual's* recipe for uncooked salad
mayonnaise is quite unusual; it calls for the expected egg, oil,
and vinegar, but also adds flour, a mashed hard-boiled egg, and
6 tbsp melted butter! I wouldn't recommend these additions. But
I do recommend the chervil, tarragon, and endive, as well as the
marigold and nasturtium blossoms, which were all in the original
recipe.

The peach season now extends from the middle of July to late
September. All through that period you can get fine peaches, but
the early varieties, especially any with the name Havens, are the
tastiest and the most fragrant. Their flesh is even-textured and
has a blush tone. Nothing is simpler—or more delicious or more
elegant—than sliced peaches with blueberries or raspberries and
sprigs of mint served in a glass bowl along with a pitcher of thick
clotted cream.

2 quarts cold homemade beef
   stock (see basic recipes)
¾ lb lean ground beef
1 medium carrot, diced
1 medium onion, chopped
1 stalk celery, chopped
1 leek, chopped
1 cup canned tomatoes
3 egg whites, slightly beaten
2 stalks parsley
8 peppercorns, crushed
½ tsp fresh chopped thyme or
   ¼ tsp dried crushed thyme
1 bay leaf
1 clove garlic, chopped
3 tbsp finely chopped chives

Chilled Consommé with Chives

Pour the stock into a large pot.

Mix together the rest of the ingredients and stir into the cold stock. Bring slowly to the boil, stirring every 5 minutes. As soon as the stock reaches the boiling point, reduce heat and simmer without stirring for 1 ½ hours.

Ladle the stock through a colander lined with rinsed cheesecloth into a clean saucepan.

Taste. Add more salt if necessary. Pour into glasses and chill to set. Sprinkle chives over each serving.

Marinade:
⅔ cup oil
3 tbsp lemon juice
1 tsp chopped fresh dill
¼ cup finely chopped parsley
1 tsp chopped fresh chervil
1 tsp finely chopped chives
½ tsp chopped fresh tarragon
1 ½ tsp salt
¼ tsp freshly ground pepper
¼ tsp dry mustard

Poaching Liquid:
12 cups cold water
2 tbsp lemon juice
6 peppercorns
1 tsp salt
1 bay leaf
1 onion, sliced

Fish and Shellfish:
1 live lobster, about 2 lbs
3 lbs firm fish fillets, e.g.
   halibut, cod, sole, haddock
¼ lb medium shimps

Garnish:
1 head bib lettuce, mild endive,
   romaine, or curly leaf lettuce,
   or a mixture
2-4 hard-boiled eggs
1 medium cucumber
12 marigold or nasturtium
   flowers

Herbed Mayonnaise:
1 cup homemade mayonnaise
   (see basic recipes)
1 tsp finely chopped fresh dill
1 tsp finely chopped chives
1 tsp finely chopped parsley
¼ tsp grated lemon peel

Fish Salad with Herbed Mayonnaise

Combine all the ingredients for the marinade. Reserve.

Place all the ingredients for the poaching liquid in a large saucepan. Bring to the boil, then reduce heat and simmer 10 minutes. Bring back to the boil and plunge the lobster in headfirst. Boil 15 minutes. Remove the lobster and reserve.

Reduce the heat, add the fish, and simmer gently until cooked, about 8-10 minutes. Remove and reserve.

Boil the shrimps 5 minutes in the same liquid. Remove and reserve.

While the lobster is still warm, remove the meat, leaving the claw meat whole and cutting the rest into ½″ slices. Place in a bowl with ¼ cup of the marinade. Toss gently, cover, and refrigerate 2 hours.

Break the fish into 1″ pieces, place in a bowl, and pour on ½ cup of the marinade. Cover and refrigerate 2 hours.

Remove the shell and black vein from the shrimps. Place in a small bowl, pour on the rest of the marinade, toss, and refrigerate 2 hours.

To serve, line a large platter with the lettuce. Combine the ingredients for the herbed mayonnaise, place in a bowl, and centre on the lettuce-lined platter. Quarter the eggs and slice the cucumber very thin. Reserve. Using a slotted spoon, remove the fish and shellfish from the marinade. Arrange the fish and shellfish around the mayonnaise, placing the lobster claws and shrimps decoratively on the top. Garnish with the cucumber, eggs, and flowers.

1 package active dry yeast (2 tsp)
1 tsp brown sugar
½ cup lukewarm water
1 cup milk
1 tsp salt
2 tbsp brown sugar
2 tbsp butter
1 ½ cups graham flour
2-2 ½ cups all-purpose or unbleached hard white flour
melted butter

Graham Flour Finger Rolls with Sweet Butter

Dissolve the yeast and the 1 tsp brown sugar in the lukewarm water. Let stand 10 minutes in a warm spot.

Scald the milk and combine with the salt, the 2 tbsp brown sugar, and the 2 tbsp butter in a large mixing bowl. Stir just enough to melt the butter. Let cool to lukewarm. Add the yeast mixture.

Beat in the graham flour, using an electric mixer if possible. Add the all-purpose or unbleached white flour as long as it is easy to beat in. Turn out onto a generously floured board and continue to knead in as much of the rest of the flour as is needed to make an unsticky dough. Knead. When the dough is smooth and elastic, after about 10 minutes of vigorous kneading, form into a smooth ball. Place in a large, well-greased bowl, turning over to grease all sides. Cover with a damp cloth. Let rise in a warm spot (a just-warmed oven is ideal) until double in bulk, about 1-1 ½ hours.

Punch the dough down to original size. Divide into 24 even pieces. Form into balls and roll into uniform finger shapes. Place 2″ apart on a greased baking sheet. Cover lightly and let rise in a warm spot until double in bulk, about 1-1 ½ hours.

Bake at 375 degrees for 15-20 minutes. Remove from the oven. For soft rolls, brush the tops with melted butter. Cool on a rack.

6 cups peach slices (Havens are good for this)
1 cup blueberries (wild if possible)
or
1 cup red or black raspberries
or
2 cups cantaloupe or honeydew balls
¼ cup white sugar
1 tbsp brandy, rum, port, or kirsch
12 sprigs of tender mint

Summer Fruit Bowl with Mint Leaves

Place the peaches in a glass bowl. Sprinkle on the other fruit. Blueberries and raspberries are especially good because of their colours. Add the sugar and liquor. Lift the fruit up gently with a spoon in order to let the sugar and liquor filter through the fruit. Cover well. Chill at least 1 hour. Remove from the refrigerator and let stand 20 minutes covered. Uncover and poke the mint sprigs around the top of the salad.

Serve with clotted cream (see below).

2 blades of mace or ¼ tsp
   ground mace
1 tsp rose water or vanilla
⅓ cup milk
1 egg, well beaten
1 ¼ cups heavy cream

Clotted Cream

Simmer the mace, rose water, and milk for 5 minutes. Cool. Strain first into the egg and then into the cream, which is in the top of a double boiler. Place over lightly boiling water. Heat slowly to 165 degrees (just above scalding). Pour into a dish and chill undisturbed for 24 hours.

hot water
3 tbsp tea, Earl Grey's is
   excellent
3 mint leaves
6 cups boiling water
6 tbsp simple syrup (see
   below)
1 lemon, sliced
ice cubes

Simple Syrup:
1 cup white sugar
1 cup water

Iced Russian Tea

Heat a jug or large teapot with the hot water. Pour out water and add the tea and mint leaves to the jug. Pour in the boiling water. Steep 6 minutes. Strain into a large pitcher. Cool and chill. To serve, place 1 tbsp simple syrup into each glass, add a slice of lemon and 3 ice cubes, fill the glass with tea, and stir. This tea will be clear and fragrant. More simple syrup and lemon may be added if desired.

   Bring the sugar and water to the boil, stirring to dissolve the sugar. Boil 1 minute. Cool.

Lobster Dinner

Mushroom and Herb Stuffed Tomatoes

Boiled Lobster with Drawn Butter and Lemon
Green Beans with Mint
Homemade White Bread

Gooseberry Fool
or
Raspberry and Red Currant Summer Pudding

Suggested wines:
chilled dry white or rosé

Lobster fishing began well over 100 years ago in Canada, but it was on a relatively small scale until about 1870, when rich inshore lobster fishing grounds were discovered. These meant an incredible increase in the quantity of lobster available. One hundred million pounds were landed in 1885, but such enormous catches reduced the stock so much that by 1918 only twenty-seven million pounds were taken. Now the catch is between thirty and forty million pounds a year, and each locality has a limited season to ensure a continued supply of lobster.

The simplest but best way of cooking lobster is to boil it.

Gooseberries have gone out of style needlessly. Gooseberry bushes were once a stock item in everyone's garden, and the berries were made into jams, jellies, pies, and puddings. I'm suggesting a summer dessert in the English tradition for this distinctive tasting berry: gooseberry fool, a combination of fruit and whipped cream.

6 large or 12 small bright red
  tomatoes
½ to ¾ tsp salt
1 lb white button mushrooms
3 tbsp lemon juice
½ cup olive oil
1 tsp salt
½ tsp freshly ground pepper
½ tsp dry mustard
2 tbsp finely chopped parsley
1 tbsp finely chopped chives or
  green onion
½ tsp dried crushed basil or 1
  tsp chopped fresh basil
½ tsp dried crushed marjoram
  or 1 tsp chopped fresh
  marjoram
1 small clove garlic, crushed

Garnish:
lettuce
parsley

Mushroom and Herb Stuffed Tomatoes

Cut an opening 1"-1 ½" in the stem end of the tomatoes, depending on the size of the tomatoes. Remove seeds and pulp, and salt lightly with the ½-¾ tsp salt. Turn over and leave to drain for 1 hour.

Meanwhile, slice the mushrooms into very thin slices. Combine all the rest of the ingredients and pour over the mushrooms. Toss lightly and marinate for 1 hour.

Fill tomatoes with mushroom salad. Distribute the dressing equally. Arrange on a platter, lined with lettuce leaves and garnished with parsley.

---

boiling water
2 bay leaves
1 tbsp salt
½ tsp peppercorns
six 1-1 ½ lb live lobsters
½ lb butter, melted
3 lemons cut in wedges,
  seeded

Boiled Lobster with Drawn Butter and Lemon

Bring to the boil two 8- or 10-quart pots of water large enough to cover the lobster. Add the bay leaves, salt, and peppercorns. Boil 5 minutes. Plunge the lobsters headfirst into the boiling water. Boil 15-20 minutes.

Serve with individual pots of melted butter, lots of lemon wedges, and thick slices of hot, homemade white bread (see basic recipes at end of book).

Green Beans with Mint

1 ½ lbs green (or yellow) beans
boiling water
1 tsp salt
2 tbsp butter, melted
2 tsp lemon juice
1 tsp very finely chopped mint

Top and tail beans. Wash. Place in a saucepan of boiling water. Reduce heat and simmer beans until tender, 12-15 minutes, or steam over boiling water 15-18 minutes or until tender. Drain. Sprinkle with salt. Combine butter, lemon juice, and mint. Pour over the beans. Toss to coat all the beans. Arrange beans parallel in a preheated serving dish.

Gooseberry Fool

1 quart gooseberries (5 cups)
2 tbsp orange juice
1 cup white sugar
2 cups heavy cream

Top and tail gooseberries. Place the gooseberries and orange juice in a saucepan over low heat. Cover and cook 30-40 minutes or until the berries are tender. Stir and mash them as they cook. Add sugar. Simmer uncovered until it dissolves. Taste, add more sugar if desired. Pass through a sieve. Chill thoroughly.

Just before serving, whip the cream. Gently fold the chilled gooseberry purée into the cream, leaving swirled traces of cream and fruit. Pour into a glass compote or bowl. Serve.

Raspberry and Red Currant Summer Pudding

1 ½ pints ripe red raspberries
1 cup red currants, cleaned off
the stems
1 cup white sugar
8-10 very thin slices of
homemade white bread (see
basic recipes)
whipped cream (see basic
recipes)

Pick over the raspberries carefully, removing any that show signs of mold. Combine with the currants and sugar in a heavy-bottomed saucepan. Let stand 1 hour to start the juices running. Place over medium heat 5 minutes to dissolve the sugar. Stir gently. The fruit should now be very juicy but should preserve its shape and colour.

In the meantime, cut the crusts from the bread. Line the bottom and sides of a 4-cup round bowl with the slices of bread, overlapping them slightly. Leave 2 slices for the top.

Spoon the fruit into the lined mould. It should fill the mould completely. Cut the remaining bread to fit over the fruit. Set a plate over the top, and weigh it down with a heavy object. Refrigerate 24 hours. The fruit syrup will have saturated the bread. Turn out onto a large plate, preferably white to show off the colour of the pudding. Serve with a bowl of lightly sweetened whipped cream.

Outdoor Eating German Style

Shrimps in Dill

Roasted Pig Tails and Ribs
Hot Potato Salad
Marinated Green Bean and Onion Salad

Assortment of:
Pickled Onions
Dill Pickles
Indian Pickles
Ridgetown Corn Relish

Hot Cornbread

Bing Cherries with Cream Cheese Dip

Many Mennonites came to Upper Canada around 1800, attracted by the prospect of good, inexpensive land and the security of continuing British citizenship. The first arrivals settled northeast of Toronto around Markham; later arrivals settled in Waterloo County. In many ways, the Mennonites have preserved to the present day a distinctly rural tradition of cooking, which features lots of sour cream, smoked meat (especially pork), nourishing soups, and excellent baked goods.

Their cooking has had considerable influence on the people around them. In the city of Kitchener, for instance, no picnic is complete without barbecued pig tails and ribs and the traditional hot potato salad. Included also in this menu is a marinated fresh bean salad from the 1914 *Canadian Family Cook Book*.

For the pickles and relishes, see the preserves section at the end of the book.

Shrimps in Dill

1 lb fresh medium shrimps
1 strip lemon peel
boiling water
3 tbsp lemon juice
1 tbsp oil
1 tbsp finely chopped parsley
2 tbsp finely chopped dill
1 green onion, finely sliced
1 small clove garlic, finely
   chopped
¼ tsp salt
¼ tsp freshly ground pepper
1 ½ cups sliced mushroom
   caps
1 tbsp white wine vinegar
½ tsp chopped fresh tarragon
¼ tsp salt
⅛ tsp freshly ground pepper
1 cup homemade mayonnaise
   (see basic recipes)
6 lettuce leaves
2 hard-boiled eggs, sliced
½ cucumber, sliced

Drop the shrimps and lemon peel into boiling water. Boil 5 minutes over medium heat. Drain. Discard the lemon. Shell the shrimps and remove the black vein. Place in a bowl with the lemon juice, oil, parsley, dill, onion, garlic, ¼ tsp salt, and ¼ tsp pepper. Toss gently, cover, and refrigerate 2 hours.

At the same time, combine the mushrooms, vinegar, tarragon, and the rest of the salt and pepper. Toss, cover, and refrigerate 2 hours.

To serve, place a lettuce leaf on each plate. Drain the shrimps and mushrooms. Combine both with the mayonnaise. Spoon mixture onto the lettuce leaves and garnish with the egg and cucumber.

Roasted Pig Tails and Ribs

2 ½-3 lbs pig tails, tail end
   removed
3-4 lbs meaty spare-ribs

Sauce:
1 ½ tsp salt
⅓ tsp freshly ground pepper
1 ½ tsp paprika
1 ½ tsp dry mustard
1 ½ tbsp brown sugar, white
   sugar, honey, or molasses
1 ½ tbsp Worcestershire sauce
¾ cup ketchup or chili sauce
   (see preserves section)
¾ cup water
⅓ cup cider vinegar
⅔ cup very finely minced
   onions
2 cloves garlic, minced

Place pig tails, fat side up, on a rack in an open roasting pan. Bake 2 hours at 300 degrees. Drain off the fat.

Meanwhile cut the ribs into individual portions of 3-4 ribs. Cover and bake 45 minutes at 300 degrees. Drain off the fat.

Combine the ingredients for the sauce. Simmer 10 minutes.

Lay the tails and ribs in the bottom of an open roasting pan. Spoon the sauce over. Return to the oven and continue cooking for another hour. Spoon on more sauce periodically so that they are well coated.

To barbecue the meat outside, preroast in the oven as directed. Then lay pieces on the outside grill, paint with the sauce, and grill till succulently brown and crisp, turning and brushing on more sauce periodically.

4 slices lean bacon
½ cup finely chopped onions
¼ cup chopped celery
1 tbsp flour
¼ cup hot water
½ cup heavy cream
2 tbsp boiled dressing (see basic recipes)
1 tbsp vinegar
½ tsp salt
¼ tsp freshly ground pepper
4 cups diced, hot, boiled potatoes
1 tbsp finely chopped parsley
1 tsp finely chopped chives
additional heavy cream (optional)
2 hard-boiled eggs, sliced

Hot Potato Salad

Cook bacon over medium heat until crisp. Remove and crumble. Drain off all fat except 1 tbsp, return to medium heat, add onions and celery. Stir in flour to coat the vegetables. Add water, stir and cook till thickened. Remove from the heat and blend in the cream, boiled dressing, vinegar, salt, and pepper. Pour over the potatoes in a large bowl. Add the parsley and chives. Mix well to blend flavours. Add more cream if desired, taste, add salt if desired. Sprinkle crumbled bacon on top and garnish with the sliced hard-boiled eggs.

1 ½ medium onions
cold water
1 ¾ lbs green beans

Dressing:
2 tbsp oil
6 tbsp vinegar
2 tsp white sugar
¾ tsp salt
¼ tsp freshly ground pepper

Garnish:
2 hard-boiled eggs, sliced
1 stalk celery, chopped fine
2 tbsp finely chopped chives

Marinated Green Bean and Onion Salad

Peel and slice onions thinly. Cover with cold water. Set aside for 2 hours. Drain onions, press water out with paper towels.

Steam beans 15-20 minutes or boil beans 12-15 minutes until tender but still slightly crisp. Drain.

Combine oil, vinegar, sugar, salt, and pepper. Pour over the beans while still warm. Toss, let cool. Add the onions and toss again.

To serve, place in a large bowl, slice the eggs over the centre of the beans, arrange the celery around the edges, and sprinkle with the chives.

1 cup sifted all-purpose flour
¼ cup white sugar
1 tbsp baking powder
¾ tsp salt
¾ cup cornmeal
1 egg, well beaten
1 cup milk
2 tbsp melted bacon fat or
   butter, cooled

Hot Cornbread

Sift together the flour, sugar, baking powder, and salt. Mix in the cornmeal.

Combine the well-beaten egg, milk, and fat. Add to the dry ingredients, stirring just enough to incorporate the flour.

Pour into a well greased cake tin 10″ x 14″. Bake at 425 degrees for 25-30 minutes or until done.

¾ cup cream cheese (European
   style if possible)
1 ½ tbsp white sugar
1 ½ tsp vanilla, brandy, or
   kirsch
⅓ cup heavy cream
2-3 quarts Bing cherries

Bing Cherries with Cream Cheese Dip

Mash the cheese up till it is smooth. European style cream cheese is not only smoother and softer but also tastier than the sort generally sold in packages. Beat in the sugar and the vanilla and gradually the heavy cream. Add more cream if a thinner dip is desired. Pour into a bowl. Centre on a platter or tray and surround with washed, unpitted, unstemmed Bing cherries.

Countryside Picnic

Cold Mustard Roasted Chicken
Traditional Potato Salad
Pickled Eggs

Marinated Zucchini and Pepper Salad

Watermelon
Black Pepper Spice Cake

Classic Lemonade

Suggested wine:
chilled white or light red

In the summer, riding and boating parties take the place of dancing. There are always regular pic-nics, each party contributing their share of eatables and drinkables to the general stock. They commonly select some pretty island in the bay, or shady retired spot on the main land, for the general rendezvous, where they light a fire, boil their kettles, and cook the vegetables to eat with their cold prog [food, victuals], which usually consists of hams, fowls, meat pies, cold joints of meat, and abundance of tarts and cakes, while the luxury of ice is conveyed in a blanket at the bottom of one of the boats. (Suzanna Moodie, *Life in the Clearings,* 1853)

one 4-lb roasting chicken (or
   capon)
1 medium onion
sprig of fresh marjoram or ¼ tsp
   dried crushed marjoram or
   sprig of fresh thyme or ¼ tsp
   dried crushed thyme
¼ tsp freshly ground pepper
3 tbsp soft butter
1 tsp dry mustard
½ tsp dried crushed summer
   savory or 1 tsp chopped fresh
   summer savory
¼ tsp freshly ground pepper
2 tbsp melted butter
1 tsp salt

Cold Mustard Roasted Chicken

Wipe the chicken with a damp cloth. Quarter the onion and place it in the cavity of the chicken with the marjoram and the first ¼ tsp pepper. Skewer the opening and truss the chicken. Dry the chicken. Make a paste of the soft butter, mustard, summer savory, and the rest of the pepper. Place the chicken breast up on a rack in an open roasting pan. Smear the paste all over the chicken. Insert meat thermometer in the thigh. Roast at 325 degrees, 30 minutes per pound. Baste periodically, initially using the melted butter, then accumulated pan juices. The chicken is ready when the thermometer registers 190 degrees (about 2 hours). Remove from the oven and salt. Cool and chill.

6 medium potatoes, washed
   but not peeled
boiling water
1 tsp salt
2 tbsp finely chopped onion
⅓ cup finely chopped celery
2 tbsp finely chopped parsley
1 tbsp finely chopped chives
2 hard-boiled eggs, chopped
2 tbsp chopped sweet green or
   red pepper (optional)
2 tbsp chopped almonds or
   walnuts (optional)
2 tbsp chopped sweet pickle
   (optional)

Dressing:
⅔ cup boiled dressing (see
   basic recipes)
⅔ cup heavy cream
¼ cup sour cream
1 tsp salt
½ tsp freshly ground pepper

Garnish:
2 hard-boiled eggs, sliced
2-3 pickled beets

Traditional Potato Salad

Boil potatoes until tender, about 20 minutes, in the boiling water and first tsp salt. Drain. Shake dry a few seconds over the heat, remove. Cool. Peel and dice. Combine with the rest of the salad ingredients.

   Blend together the dressing ingredients. Stir into the salad. Taste, add more salt if necessary. Chill. Garnish with sliced hard-boiled eggs and/or slices of pickled beets.

8 medium eggs
water
1 cup white wine vinegar
½ cup water
¾ cup white sugar
1 tsp salt
1 tsp peppercorns, cracked

Pickled Eggs

Place eggs in a saucepan, cover with cold water. Cover the saucepan. Bring to the boil over high heat. Remove immediately from the heat. Let stand 20 minutes. Drain. Cool and peel under cold running water. Place eggs in a glass container. Bring the rest of the ingredients to the boil. Boil 1 minute. Cool and pour over eggs. Leave at least 2 days before eating.

Another good and simple way to pickle eggs is to drop hard-boiled eggs into the liquid left from a jar of pickled beets or icicle pickles.

12 small tender young zucchini
boiling water
½ tsp salt
1 green pepper
½ sweet red pepper

Dressing:
½ cup olive oil
2 tbsp lemon juice
½ tsp salt
¼ tsp freshly ground pepper
1 tsp chopped fresh basil
2 tbsp finely chopped parsley
2 green onions, chopped finely
1 clove garlic, chopped finely
1 tsp finely chopped capers

Garnish:
lettuce leaves, preferably
    romaine or curly leaf lettuce

Marinated Zucchini and Pepper Salad

Place the zucchini and the ½ tsp salt into a saucepan. Cover with boiling water, put on the lid, bring to the boil, then reduce heat and simmer 8 minutes. The zucchini should still be firm. Drain, cut in half lengthwise, and lay in a shallow dish. Remove the core and seed from the green and red peppers, cut into strips lengthwise, and lay over the zucchini.

Combine all the rest of the ingredients except the lettuce and pour over the vegetables. Cover and refrigerate 3-4 hours. Spoon the dressing over the vegetables periodically.

To serve, line a platter with the lettuce leaves, lay the zucchini and pepper strips attractively along the middle of the leaves, and pour over any remaining dressing. Serve immediately.

¾ cup shortening
¾ cup firmly packed brown
   sugar
1 cup white sugar
3 eggs
1 tsp vanilla
2 ¼ cups sifted cake flour
1 tsp baking powder
¾ tsp soda
1 tsp salt
¾ tsp ground cinnamon
¾ tsp ground cloves
½ tsp freshly grated nutmeg
¼ tsp freshly ground black
   pepper
1 cup buttermilk

Black Pepper Spice Cake

Prepare pans. Grease three 8″ x 9″ layer pans. Line the bottoms with rounds of greased waxed paper.

Cream the shortening until it is light and fluffy. Gradually beat in the sugar. Add the eggs one at a time, beating well after each addition. Mix in the vanilla.

Sift together the flour, baking powder, soda, salt, and spices. Add them in 3 parts alternately with the buttermilk in 2 parts to the creamed mixture. Begin and end with the dry ingredients.

Pour into the greased pans. Drop the pans 2-3 inches onto the counter or table. Gently push the batter out to the edges, forming a slight depression in the middle.

Bake at 350 degrees for 25-30 minutes or until a skewer inserted in the middle comes out clean.

Remove from oven. Cool 10 minutes. Invert on racks and cool thoroughly.

Fill with plum and raisin conserve (see preserves section at end of book). Ice with caramel icing (see below).

---

1 cup firmly packed brown
   sugar
2 tbsp butter
¼ cup light cream
2 tsp rum
2-2 ½ cups sifted icing sugar

Caramel Icing for Spice Cake

Mix the brown sugar, butter, and cream in a heavy-bottomed saucepan. Stir over low heat until the sugar dissolves. Bring rapidly to the boil and boil without stirring 2 minutes. Remove from heat. Cool to lukewarm. Place the pan in ice water.

Add the rum and enough of the icing sugar to make it thick enough to spread easily. Spread over the cake.

---

1 cup lemon juice (4 lemons)
½ cup orange juice (1 large
   orange)
¾ cup white sugar
4 cups cold water
18 ice cubes

Classic Lemonade

Stir the juice and sugar together in a large pitcher. Add the water and ice cubes. Stir thoroughly and chill.

Broiled Whitefish Supper

Broiled Whitefish with Mushroom Mayonnaise
Spinach with Rosemary
Hot Potato Scones

Choice of:
Peach Sherbet
Red Currant Ice
Summer Fruit Ice Creams

Suggested wine:
chilled dry white

Nothing captures the flavour of summer like fresh fruit ices or homemade ice cream. The earliest recipe for ice cream appeared in the 1831 *Cook Not Mad*. We know ices were sold in York as early as 1833, because Thomas Hamilton, an English visitor, was "rather surprised to observe an affiche intimating that ice creams were to be had within. The weather being hot, I entered, and found the master of the establishment to be an Italian. I never ate better ices at Grange's."

Ices and ice creams long remained an esoteric specialty, well beyond the means of most people, for the method of manufacture was complicated: one bowl containing the cream mixture surrounded by ice and salt in a second, larger bowl. The maker had to beat the mixture by hand and shake it up and down in the larger bowl. The invention of the hand-cranked freezer in 1846 by the American Nancy Johnson made this process much easier, and versions of this invention remained the method of making homemade ice cream until mechanical refrigeration became common.

Basic ice cream is of two sorts. The first sort is called French, because it is made with a rich egg custard combined with cream and flavouring. It is pale yellow in colour. The second, simpler sort is made just with cream, sugar, and flavouring. Of course, sweetened fruits, nuts, syrup, etc., can easily be added to either sort to produce ice cream "flavours." Most recipes suggest making these additions just as the cream begins to be a frozen mush. Although ice creams can be made in freezer trays, a crank-turned ice cream maker gives a finer, creamier texture.

Fruit ices or sherbets, on the other hand, can be made in the freezing compartment of a refrigerator. The texture is quite good if you remember to beat the fruit purée thoroughly just as it begins to freeze. Also, be sure to eat homemade ices and ice creams within days of making, for without preservatives they soon lose their flavour and become icy.

2 whitefish, about 2-3 lbs each, boned and scaled (pickerel, lake trout, or black bass can be substituted)
2 cloves garlic, chopped very fine
¾ cup finely chopped onion (1 medium)
½ tsp freshly ground pepper
¼ cup melted butter
3 tbsp lemon juice
1 tsp grated lemon rind
2 tbsp finely minced celery leaves
½ cup finely chopped mushroom stalks
2 stalks chopped parsley or chervil
3 tbsp melted butter
2 tbsp lemon juice
salt

Garnish:
parsley sprigs

Broiled Whitefish with Mushroom Mayonnaise

Wipe the fish with a damp cloth. Do not wash. Combine the garlic, onion, pepper, ¼ cup melted butter, 3 tbsp lemon juice, and lemon rind. Rub the fish all over, inside and out, with this mixture.

Combine the celery leaves, mushroom, and the chopped parsley or chervil, and put half of the mixture in the cavity of each fish.

Place in a shallow pan. Broil 4″ from the heat, basting with the 3 tbsp melted butter and the 2 tbsp lemon juice. Cook about 15-20 minutes or until the fish flakes easily. You do not need to turn the fish over. Lower the broiling pan if the skin begins to burn before the fish are cooked. Place on a preheated platter. Pour pan juices over the fish.

Serve hot, garnished with parsley.

¾ cup very finely sliced mushroom caps
1 tsp lemon juice
1 cup homemade mayonnaise (see basic recipes)
1 tsp finely chopped parsley
1 tbsp capers

Mushroom Mayonnaise

Sprinkle mushrooms with lemon juice. Let stand while you prepare the mayonnaise. Combine mayonnaise with the mushrooms, lemon juice, parsley, and capers. Chill 15 minutes to mix flavours. Serve with broiled fish.

2 lbs spinach
½ tsp chopped fresh rosemary
¼ cup finely chopped green
   onions
¾ tsp salt
2 tbsp butter
1 tsp lemon juice

Spinach with Rosemary

Wash the spinach in several changes of cold water. Drain. Remove the coarse stems and heavy ribs. Place in a large sauce-pan. No water is needed as the drops on the leaves provide plenty. Add the rosemary and green onion, tossing lightly to distribute among the leaves. Cover and cook over medium heat 3-4 minutes or just until the spinach is wilted. Shake the pot frequently during the cooking. Drain. Toss with the salt, butter, and lemon juice. Serve immediately.

1 ½ cups sifted all-purpose
     flour
1 tbsp baking powder
1 tsp salt
2 tbsp shortening
½ cup cold mashed potatoes
½ cup milk (approximately)

Hot Potato Scones

Sift together the flour, baking powder, and salt.
   Cut in the shortening with a pastry blender or two knives.
   Add potatoes, mix well.
   Add enough milk to make a soft dough.
   Roll out ½″ thick on a lightly floured board. Cut out biscuits.
Place on lightly floured baking sheets.
   Bake at 400 degrees until well risen and golden brown, about 12-15 minutes. Remove from the baking sheets and serve while still hot. Yield: about 24, depending upon size.

¾ cup white sugar
1 cup water
1 ½ cups sliced peeled stoned
     peaches
2 tbsp lemon juice
⅛ tsp salt

Peach Sherbet

Combine the sugar and water. Boil together 5 minutes. Cool.
   Sieve or purée the peaches in a food mill or blender. Mix in the lemon juice and salt. Stir together the cooled syrup and the fruit.
   Pour into cake pans or freezer trays. Freeze until mushy, 1-1 ½ hours. Transfer to a chilled mixing bowl and beat with an electric beater till smooth and creamy. Spoon into containers and return to the freezer. This sherbet is best if eaten before frozen too hard.

1 cup red currants, washed and
  stemmed
½ cup water
1 ¼ cups water
1 cup white sugar
2 egg whites

Red Currant Ice

Put currants and ½ cup water into a saucepan. Cover and simmer over moderate heat 15 minutes. Push through a sieve. Measure out 1 ¼ cups currant juice and purée.

Boil together the 1 ¼ cups water and sugar for 5 minutes. Cool slightly and combine with the fruit purée.

Pour into cake pans or shallow freezer trays and freeze until mushy, 1-1 ½ hours.

Beat the egg whites till stiff but not dry.

Empty the semi-frozen purée into a chilled bowl and beat until smooth and creamy. Combine gently with the egg whites. Spoon into containers and return to the freezer. Ideal if served before frozen hard.

---

1 pint wild blueberries
or
1 pint ripe red raspberries
or
2 cups sliced, peeled peaches
½ cup white sugar
pinch of salt
2 ½ cups heavy cream

Summer Fruit Ice Creams

Crush the blueberries or raspberries lightly.

Add the sugar and salt to whichever of the fruits being used. Mix in well. Cover and refrigerate 2 hours to mature the flavour.

Pour the cream into the can of the churn freezer. Cover. Surround the can to within 1″ of the lid with layers of crushed ice and salt, 3 parts ice to 1 part salt (use coarse street salt). Pack down as firmly as possible. Add more ice and salt as needed to maintain the level.

Turn the crank slowly until the cream is frozen-mushy, about 10 minutes. Add the chilled, sugared fruit. Continue churning, turning the crank more quickly until freezing is accomplished.

Remove the can, wipe off the salt. Take out the dasher and pack down the ice cream. Store in the freezing compartment of the refrigerator 1-2 hours or until serving time. This storage improves the texture of the ice cream, but it can be eaten immediately.

Summer Weekend Breakfast

Cantaloupe Wedges

Buttermilk Blueberry Pancakes
Crisp Bacon
Maple Butter

Todmorden Cinnamon Coffee Cake
Ginger Pear Marmalade and
Black Currant Jelly

Coffee

This breakfast menu is nice for a lazy weekend morning at home or for a special breakfast with company at the cottage. It's an opportunity to serve together some of the summer's fruit jams and jellies and fresh blueberries at their peak—a wonderful combination of tastes. The whipped maple butter for the pancakes is a combination of grated maple sugar, maple syrup, and butter.

Buttermilk combined with soda in the pancakes makes for a fine, smooth light texture.

For ginger pear marmalade and black currant jelly, see the preserves section at the end of the book.

1 medium, ripe, fragrant
   cantaloupe
1 lime, thinly sliced
powdered ginger

Cantaloupe Wedges

Chill the cantaloupe, cut into wedges, remove the seeds. Make 3 lengthwise cuts in each wedge and 7-8 crosswise cuts. Cut along just above the rind the length of the wedge. The cantaloupe should now be in bite-sized pieces.

Serve garnished with lime slices or very lightly sprinkled with powdered ginger.

1 ½ cups sifted all-purpose
   flour
1 tsp baking powder
½ tsp soda
3 tbsp white sugar
¾ tsp salt
1 egg, lightly beaten
1 ½ cups buttermilk
3 tbsp melted butter, cooled
1 cup fresh wild blueberries

Buttermilk Blueberry Pancakes

Sift together the dry ingredients.

Combine the egg, buttermilk, and melted butter. Add to the dry ingredients, mixing just long enough to incorporate the flour. Quickly stir in the blueberries.

Cook on a hot, lightly greased griddle or frying pan. Turn when the bubbles break and batter does not fill the holes. Cook on the other side until the pancake evens out. Yield: 12 medium pancakes.

¾-1 lb lean bacon, sliced

Crisp Bacon

Fry the bacon over moderate heat until crisp. Drain off the fat. Pat the bacon between paper towels to remove excess fat.

½ cup sweet butter
¼ cup grated maple sugar
½ cup maple syrup
⅛ tsp freshly grated nutmeg

Maple Butter

Whip butter until light and fluffy. Continue beating as you add the maple sugar and syrup. Pack into a pretty bowl. Sprinkle with nutmeg. Serve a large spoonful on each pancake.

Todmorden Cinnamon Coffee Cake

Batter:

½ cup butter
½ cup white sugar
2 eggs
1 tsp vanilla
1 tsp baking soda
1 cup sour cream
1 ½ cups sifted all-purpose
   flour
1 ½ tsp baking powder
¼ tsp salt

Topping:

¼ cup white sugar
1 tbsp ground cinnamon
2 tbsp chopped nuts

Cream the butter till light and fluffy. Beat in the sugar. Add the eggs one at a time, beating after each addition. Stir in the vanilla.

Dissolve the soda in the sour cream.

Sift together the flour, baking powder, and salt.

Add the dry ingredients in 3 parts alternately with the sour cream and soda in 2 parts to the beaten mixture.

Combine the ingredients for the topping.

Spoon half the batter into a well greased 9" x 9" cake tin. Sprinkle with half the topping, add remaining batter, and sprinkle with the rest of the topping.

Bake at 350 degrees for 25 minutes or until it comes away from the sides. Serve while still warm.

Fall

Canadian gardeners (and cooks) wonder what to *do* with all the fall vegetables. The answer right up until World War II was to feast on these foods when they were at their most succulent and to preserve as much as possible of the rest. Every family had its fruit cellar, the cool room in the basement lined with rough shelves of crocks and jars of preserves, and no one regarded a bulging fruit cellar as a mark of either stinginess or poverty. On the contrary, women took pride in the clarity of their jelly, the fresh taste of their preserved pears and plums, and the variety and quality of their pickles. And it was a just pride: not everyone can make good pickles, for instance! The retention of the colour and crispness is a matter of no little skill, and has to do with freshness, timing, temperature, quantities—in short, care and experience.

It also has to do with taste. For example, although dill pickles are fairly simple to preserve in quantity, they don't go with everything. They may be terrific with cold meats, but they do not complement a loin of pork the way spiced fruits do. Nor do they suit roast goose. It was necessary to be able to choose the right accent to the main course. This was not done by making a sauce, as in the French tradition, but rather by going "down cellar" to find the perfect relish or jelly or pickle. Only by preserving the succession of fruits and vegetables in their season was this choice possible. Of course, personal preferences existed, and naturally regional differences varied the choice of raw materials. But people all over the country made relishes for their food. They found that they could add the extra touch of flavour, texture, and accent to a simply cooked main course. I think they still can, and should. That is why I have included a good number of recipes for preserves at the back of this book.

At the heart of the fall season is Thanksgiving, the celebration of the harvest. Sir John A. MacDonald first made a public holiday of it in 1879, proclaiming it as "a day of general Thanksgiving to the Almighty God for the bountiful harvest with which Canada has been blessed this year." Even though this holiday was to be in the English tradition of a religious harvest festival, it was difficult for it not to be influenced by the American Thanksgiving (which commemorates the arrival of the Pilgrims in 1621). In fact, for some years our Thanksgiving actually took place in November on a Thursday! In 1900 it was switched to the first or third Monday in October, only to return to November after World War I, when Thanksgiving and Remembrance Day were celebrated as one. Finally it returned to October in 1929, and in 1957 was settled on once and for all as the second Monday in October.

We still share with the Americans the tradition of turkey, cranberries, and pumpkin pies. But it is, of course, possible to use the traditional ingredients advisedly and turn out something extraordinary. First of all, there are turkeys and turkeys. A fresh, well-hung bird is bound to be superior to a frozen one. And there are pies and pies. When properly made, there is nothing better than a good pumpkin pie. As an alternative to pie, the 1831 winter squash pudding with rose water suggested in the Thanksgiving dinner menu is a delightful delicacy. The fragrance when it is cooking is fascinating for its unusual blend of spices and flavours.

The Thanksgiving meal and the others in this section include both seasonal and traditional specialties and less well-known Canadian recipes. If there is ever a time for good and interesting Canadian cooking, it is in the fall.

Thanksgiving Dinner

Smoked Salmon
Lemon Wedges and Horse-radish

Traditional Roast Turkey
with
Oyster Stuffing and Giblet Gravy
Turnip Soufflé
Cranberry Sauce
Glazed Onions

Choice of:
Classic Pumpkin Pie
Lemon Rum Squash Pie
1831 Winter Squash Pudding with Rose Water

Suggested wine:
chilled dry white, dry red, or chilled rosé

Smoked Salmon

6 thin slices stone-ground brown bread (see basic recipes)
sweet butter
½ lb smoked salmon, sliced thinly
2 tsp capers very finely chopped
parsley
1 lemon, cut in wedges, seeded
pepper mill
grated horse-radish

Trim the crusts from the bread. Spread with butter. Cut each slice into three fingers. Lay the salmon slices on the bread, overlapping to make a generous topping. Put a sprinkle of capers along the centre. Place the salmon fingers on a serving dish, and garnish with parsley. Arrange lemon wedges among the fingers. Pass a pepper mill and horse-radish.

Because of the volume of Pacific salmon fishing, most smoked salmon for sale in Canada is from British Columbia, and is frozen before being smoked. The closest equivalent to Scotch smoked salmon, considered to be the world's finest, is East Coast salmon. The species of salmon is the same and an attempt has been made to reproduce the same hardwood smoking process.

1 fresh turkey, 12-16 lbs
1 tsp salt
stuffing (see below)
½-¾ cup soft butter
¾ tsp freshly ground pepper
cheesecloth
1 tbsp flour
salt

Traditional Roast Turkey with Oyster Stuffing and Giblet Gravy

Prepare turkey by pulling out any remaining pin feathers with tweezers and removing the oil sac at the base of the tail. Wipe the interior and neck cavities with a damp cloth. Salt cavities lightly with 1 tsp salt. Stuff neck cavity loosely with stuffing, fold the skin over, and skewer or sew opening.

Fill the body cavity loosely and skewer or sew opening. Dry bird; truss. Smear with about 4 tbsp of the butter and sprinkle with pepper. Lay breast down (ensures moist white meat) on a greased rack in an uncovered roasting pan. Drape the turkey with two layers of cheesecloth, smear with 2 tbsp butter, and place in oven, preheated to 325 degrees. Baste with melted butter initially, then occasionally with accumulated pan juices. Halfway through the cooking period, turn the turkey on its back, now placing the cheesecloth over the breast. If the marks on the breast are a worry, simply roast the turkey for the entire time on its back. The cheesecloth should cover the breast. Roast turkey 5 ¾ hours to 6 ¾ hours, approximately 25 minutes per pound, or until a meat thermometer inserted in the thigh registers 190 degrees. 45 minutes before the end of the cooking time, remove the cheesecloth and sprinkle the turkey evenly with flour. Return to the oven. Leave 15 minutes, then baste to set the crust. Baste once more before end of cooking period. Remove from the oven and place on a large platter in a warm place. Salt lightly. Let rest 10-15 minutes before carving. This resting not only allows time to prepare the gravy but also lets the meat reabsorb some of its juices. This sets the meat and makes it easier to carve.

Oyster Stuffing for Turkey

8-10 cups ¼"-½" bread cubes
   (homemade bread is best)
6 slices lean bacon, chopped
¼ cup butter
1 cup celery, chopped
1 cup onions, chopped
1 tsp dried crushed summer
   savory
1 tsp dried crushed thyme
1 tsp dried crushed sage
2 tsp salt
¼ tsp freshly ground pepper
¼ cup coarsely chopped fresh
   parsley
1 pint fresh shucked oysters in
   their own liquor

Place bread cubes on a baking sheet and toast lightly in the oven. Stir as they toast so that they brown evenly. Cool, place in a large mixing bowl.

Melt the butter over medium heat. Add the bacon, sauté lightly 5 minutes. Add the celery, onions, savory, thyme, sage, salt, and pepper. Cook until the vegetables are transparent. Do not brown.

Add the parsley. Chop each oyster into 4 pieces. Add to the herbed vegetables and continue cooking 3-4 minutes or until the oysters begin to firm up.

Combine the cooked vegetable and oyster mixture with the toasted bread. Mix thoroughly. Cool.

Giblet Gravy

neck, heart, liver, gizzard of
   turkey
1 small onion
4" piece of celery
1 small bay leaf
¼ tsp dried crushed thyme
½ tsp salt
¼ tsp freshly ground pepper
6-7 cups water or chicken stock
   (see basic recipes)
drippings
¼ cup flour
2 tbsp red currant jelly (see
   preserves section)
salt
pepper

Combine first 7 ingredients in a saucepan. Cover plus ¼ with the water. Bring to the boil. Remove scum, reduce heat, and simmer uncovered until the giblets are tender, about 1½ hours. Strain and reserve stock and giblets. Trim and chop the heart, liver, and gizzard. Reserve. Skim off fat from the drippings in the roasting pan and work flour into the pan juices with a wooden spoon. Place over medium heat. Gradually add 4 cups of the giblet stock, stirring to make a smooth sauce. More stock may be added if desired. Add the reserved chopped giblets. Add jelly, stir to melt. Taste. Adjust seasoning. Serve very hot in a preheated gravy boat.

2 lbs turnip (1 medium turnip)
2 cups lightly salted chicken
    stock (see basic recipes)
2 tbsp butter
1 tbsp brown sugar
⅛ tsp freshly ground pepper
⅛ tsp ground mace
1 tsp baking powder
2 eggs, separated
salt
3 tbsp butter
½ cup fine dry bread crumbs

Turnip Soufflé

Peel turnip, chop into ½″ cubes. Place in a saucepan with the stock. Cover. Bring to the boil. Reduce heat and simmer until tender, about 25 minutes. Drain, reserving stock for another use, such as soup. Mash the turnips very well. There should be about 3 cups. Add the 2 tbsp butter, brown sugar, pepper, mace, baking powder, and yolks of the eggs. Stir well to blend ingredients. Taste. Add salt if desired. Melt the 3 tbsp butter, add the crumbs, and sauté 3-4 minutes. Beat the egg whites till stiff but not dry. Fold into the turnip mixture. Spoon into a buttered soufflé dish. Sprinkle with the buttered crumbs. Bake at 375 degrees for 25 minutes or until lightly browned on top.

2 cups white sugar
1 ½ cups water
½ cup port
2 whole cloves
zest of ¼ orange
4 cups cranberries

Cranberry Sauce

Combine sugar, water, port, and cloves in a saucepan. Sliver the orange zest into very fine pieces. Add to the saucepan, bring to the boil, then reduce heat and simmer 5 minutes.

Remove the cloves. Add the cranberries and simmer uncovered until they pop, about 5-7 minutes. Pour into a serving dish or three 8-oz hot sterilized jars. Seal jars with melted paraffin wax. Yield: about 3 cups.

2 lbs onions (about 24 small or
    12 medium onions)
¼ cup butter
½ cup chicken stock (see basic
    recipes)
1 tsp white sugar
¼-½ tsp salt, depending on
    saltiness of chicken stock
1 tbsp finely chopped chives
1 tbsp finely chopped parsley

Glazed Onions

Peel onions. Cut a shallow X in the bottom of the onions. Melt the butter in a saucepan wide enough to accommodate the onions in one layer. Add the onions and sauté over medium heat, turning them frequently until golden on all sides (about 5 minutes).

Add the stock, sugar, and salt. Cover tightly, reduce heat to medium low, and continue cooking for about 30 minutes or until the onions are tender and the stock reduced. Length of time will depend on the size of the onions.

Shake the saucepan gently 3-4 times during the cooking period to glaze the onions on all sides.

Remove onions to a warm shallow dish. Sprinkle with chives and parsley.

1 deep 10" unbaked, unpricked
   pie shell (see basic recipes)
1 ½ cups pumpkin purée (see
   basic recipes)
¾ cup firmly packed brown
   sugar
½ tsp salt
1 ½ tsp ground cinnamon
1 ¼ tsp ground ginger
½ tsp ground cloves
½ tsp freshly grated nutmeg
3 eggs, well beaten
1 ¼ cups milk
¾ cup evaporated milk
whipped cream (see basic
   recipes)

Classic Pumpkin Pie

Refrigerate the pie shell.

Thoroughly blend all ingredients for the filling. Pour into the chilled pie shell.

Bake at 450 degrees for 10 minutes. Reduce heat to 350 degrees, continue baking 45-50 minutes longer or until the point of a knife inserted into the middle comes out clean.

Cool and serve with a bowl of sweetened whipped cream.

1 deep 10" unbaked, unpricked
   pie shell (see basic recipes)
1 ½ cups thick, mashed squash
½ cup white sugar
1 tbsp lemon juice
½ tsp grated lemon rind
¾ tsp ground ginger
¾ tsp ground cinnamon
1 tsp freshly grated nutmeg
¼ tsp salt
1 tbsp rum
¾ cup heavy cream
¼ cup molasses
2 eggs, well beaten
1 cup milk
whipped cream (see basic
   recipes)

Lemon Rum Squash Pie

Follow the recipe on the next page for the thick mashed squash.

Chill the pie shell.

Combine all the ingredients except the eggs and milk in a large bowl. Beat the eggs and the milk together, strain into the other ingredients. Blend together.

Pour into the pie shell. Bake at 450 degrees for 10 minutes, reduce heat to 350 degrees, and bake 40-50 minutes or until the tip of a knife inserted in the middle comes out clean. Cool and serve with whipped cream.

Winter Squash Pudding with Rose Water

1 medium squash, buttercup, butternut, sweetmeat, or delecta
6 cups peeled, cored, chopped cooking apples
2 tbsp lemon juice (½ lemon)
1 tsp grated lemon rind (½ lemon)
¼ cup water
6 tbsp finely crushed dry bread crumbs or cookie crumbs
1 tbsp all-purpose flour
¼ tsp ground cinnamon
2 ½ tsp freshly grated nutmeg
½ tsp salt
1 ½ cups firmly packed brown sugar
5 egg yolks, lightly beaten
2 ½ cups light cream
1 tbsp rose water
2 tbsp sherry
5 egg whites
whipped cream (see basic recipes)

Peel the squash. Remove seeds. Steam the squash until tender, about 20 minutes. Drain well and mash, sieve or blend. (Should be 3 cups of squash purée.)

Simmer the apples, lemon juice and rind, and water in a covered saucepan for 20 minutes. Uncover, simmer 10 minutes. Mash, put through a sieve or blend.

Combine the squash, apple, crumbs, flour, spices, salt, brown sugar, yolks, cream, rose water, and sherry. Taste. Add more sugar and/or spices if desired.

Beat the egg whites till stiff but not dry. Fold into the squash-apple mixture. Pour into a large buttered ovenproof dish.

Bake one hour at 350 degrees or until the custard is set in the middle.

Serve the whipped cream with the pudding. The pudding can be eaten hot, warm, or chilled.

Serves 10-12 generously.

Roast Loin of Pork with Thyme Dinner

Rich Creamed Mushroom Soup

Roast Loin of Pork with Thyme
Spiced Pears
Spiced Crab Apples
Pepper Squash Roasted with Maple Syrup and Cider

Savoy Cabbage Salad

Lattice-top Cranberry Pie

Suggested wine:
dry red

Describing the local livestock, Suzanna Moodie spoke of Canada's "race of pigs, tall and gaunt, with fierce bristling manes, that wandered about the roads and woods, seeking what they could devour, like famished wolves." In spite of this seemingly poor quality, pork continued to be the dietary mainstay of Ontario settlers. It has been estimated that in the first half of the nineteenth century, it was not uncommon for some people to eat as much as 465 pounds of pork per year. With present annual consumption more like 50 pounds per person per year, pork still stands second only to beef.

Good pork is available all year round, but it is generally more plentiful in the fall and winter. Recently pork producers have been trying to promote pork as an all-season meat, but the rich flavour seems to suit the cool months best. This meal calls for a loin, the best pork roast. A simple marination in cider with marjoram and thyme accents the flavour of the meat.

While fat on most meats is considered inferior to lean, the ½" layer of creamy fat on a loin of pork, studded with a bread crumb-parsley mixture and well basted with pan juices, cooks into an irresistible golden crust.

The spiced fruit garnish—pears and crab apples—illustrates how important preserves are to complement a simple main course. Their spicy-sweet-sour taste is just right with roast pork.

Squash, too, comes into its own in the fall. Farmers' markets and street and roadside stands all over the country sell great mounds of the many varieties of squash: dark green acorn, pepper, buttercup, golden butternut, straight or crook neck, butter, and hubbards that come in golden, green, warted, and blue. The hubbards are the giants of the family.

Squash baked in cider, maple syrup, and butter may seem peculiar, but the mingled maple and apple flavours raise baked squash to aristocratic heights. For this recipe use the small acorn or pepper varieties.

For recipes for spiced pears and spiced crab apples, see the preserves section at the end of the book.

Rich Creamed Mushroom Soup

¼ cup butter
½ cup finely chopped onions
1 clove garlic, finely chopped
2 ½ cups sliced fresh mushrooms
5 tbsp flour
4 ½ cups lightly salted chicken stock (see basic recipes)
1 small bay leaf
¼ tsp freshly ground pepper
½ tsp salt
1 cup medium cream
3 tbsp finely chopped chives

Melt the butter in a large heavy-bottomed saucepan. Add the onions and garlic. Cook over medium heat until the onions are transparent, about 3-4 minutes. Add the mushrooms. Stir well. Cook 3 minutes more. Stir in the flour, taking care to coat the vegetables. Cook 2-3 minutes. Gradually add the stock, stirring well to prevent lumps. Add the bay leaf, pepper, and salt. Bring to the boil. Reduce heat and simmer 15 minutes. Remove bay leaf. Stir in cream. Taste. Add more salt if desired. Heat through. Garnish with chives.

one 5-lb loin of pork
¾ tsp dried crushed thyme or 5
little sprigs fresh thyme
¼ tsp dried crushed marjoram
or ½ tsp chopped fresh
marjoram
¾ cup cider or white or red
wine
¾ tsp salt
¼ cup finely chopped parsley
¼ cup fine stale but not dry
bread crumbs

Gravy:
1 tbsp flour
1 cup water or chicken stock
(see basic recipes)
1 tbsp red currant jelly (see
preserves section)
salt and pepper

Roast Loin of Pork with Thyme

Lay the roast in a shallow roasting pan. Place the pieces of thyme evenly along the roast close to the bone. Sprinkle with marjoram. Pour on the cider or wine and let stand for one hour, turning the roast periodically.

Set fat side up, cover loosely with aluminum foil, and roast at 350 degrees for a total of 3 hours, approximately 35 minutes per pound or to 185 degrees on a meat thermometer.

¾ hour before the end of the cooking time remove the covering foil. Salt lightly. Combine parsley and bread crumbs. Spread onto the fat side, pressing down if necessary to make them stick. Lower heat to 325 degrees.

Return to oven and continue roasting, basting every 10 minutes with accumulated pan juices. There should be a crisp golden crust on the ouside.

Set the roast on a preheated platter in a warm place for 10-15 minutes. This allows the juices to flow back into the meat. The roast is then also easier to carve.

To make the gravy, remove all the fat from the pan juices. Blend in 1 tbsp of flour shaken up in a jar with 1 cup cold water or chicken stock. Place over medium heat, and simmer until smooth and thickened. Add the red currant jelly, season to taste, and add more liquid to desired consistency. Serve the gravy very hot in a preheated gravy boat.

3 pepper or acorn squash
1 ½ tsp salt
6 tbsp butter
6 tbsp fresh cider
½ cup maple syrup

Pepper Squash Roasted with Maple Syrup and Cider

Cut the squash in half and remove the seeds. Place in a roasting pan, sprinkle with salt, and cover. Bake at 350 degrees until almost tender, about 45 minutes. Remove cover.

Meanwhile, melt the butter and combine it with the cider and maple syrup. Brush the insides of the squash generously with this liquid. Return to the oven. Bake, continuing to brush with the basting mixture periodically until it is all used up and the squash are tender and well browned. This will take about 15-30 minutes, depending on size.

Salad:
4 cups finely sliced or chopped
    Savoy cabbage
⅓ cup finely chopped onion
½ cup finely chopped celery
¼ cup raisins cut in half
1 bright red apple, cored and
    chopped. Leave on the peel.
1 tbsp chopped sweet red or
    green pepper

Dressing:
¼ cup boiled dressing (see
    basic recipes)
¼ cup sour cream
¼ cup heavy sweet cream
¼ tsp freshly ground pepper
½ tsp mustard seed
½ tsp celery seed
½ tsp salt

Savoy Cabbage Salad

Combine all the salad ingredients in a large bowl. Blend together the ingredients for the dressing. Pour over the salad. Toss well. Best if refrigerated for 1 hour before serving. Taste. Add more salt and pepper if necessary.

---

sufficient pastry for a 2-crust 9″
    pie (see basic recipes)
3 cups cranberries
¼ cup water
2 cups white sugar
1 tbsp butter
¼ tsp ground cassia
whipped cream (see basic
    recipes)

Lattice-top Cranberry Pie

Wash the cranberries, combine with the water, and cook in a covered saucepan over moderate heat for about 10 minutes. The cranberries should have almost all "popped."

Add the sugar. Cook 10 minutes more uncovered. Taste, add more sugar if desired.

Add the butter and ground cassia. Cool while you prepare the two crusts.

Lattice:
On a piece of waxed paper, draw the circumference of the pie.

Roll out half the pastry into a rectangular shape. Cut the pastry into ½″ strips.

Weave the strips together on the piece of waxed paper, trimming them to the size of the circle. Lightly press the places where the lengthwise and crosswise strips meet.

Slip the lattice and paper into the freezer for a few minutes.

Roll out the rest of the dough for the bottom crust. Line the pie plate and fill with the cranberries. Dampen the edges of the crust. Slide the lattice over the berries. Trim the edges and flute.

Bake 15 minutes at 425 degrees. Reduce heat to 375 and bake the pie 30 minutes or until golden brown.

Duck with Wild Rice Dinner

Braised Leeks

Duck with Wild Rice and Mushrooms
Creamed Jerusalem Artichokes

Green Pepper and Endive Salad

Chocolate Almond Sponge Roll

Suggested wine:
full-bodied red

Wild rice, the feature attraction of this menu, is one of Canada's most precious culinary products. It is actually an aquatic grass, which grows from four to six feet tall. The edible seeds are purply-black, resemble coarse spruce needles, and have a slightly smokey flavour. When cooked, they puff somewhat and are snowy white inside. They are a totally natural product, nutritionally richer than domestic brown and white rice.

Wild rice grows in shallow lakes, slow-moving streams, and marshes with mud or silt bottoms, and is harvested from New Brunswick to Manitoba. In the summer months, the long grassy leaves float on the surface of the water and provide fodder for deer. In the early fall, during harvest, the matured seeds feed flocks of migrating ducks and geese.

By late August or early September, when the leaves have withered, harvest begins. This is still mainly done by Indians, who canoe through beds of rice, bend the heads of the plants over the edge of the canoe, and knock off the grains into the bottom of the canoe with a curved sharp stick. After the harvest comes the important step of drying. This was generally done by spreading the rice out in the sun or stirring it over a fire, but previously, parching was done on reed mats suspended over hot coals. The rice must be stirred to ensure complete drying. Winnowing on a breezy day finishes the preparation of wild rice. Now the rice is sold green by the Indians and dried in large driers. This long, painstaking process forcibly turns wild rice into a luxury item. It would be nice to think that it could be bought from the Indians in order to return to them a reasonable profit for their work. Attempts by the Indian cooperatives to market their own rice in the United States have so far failed because of pressure from big American companies. The Canadian market is controlled by these same companies, and they are trying to maintain this position and their control over the sources of wild rice. One cooperative in Kenora, Ontario, however, has managed to market its own product.

The rice's distinct flavour, unusual appearance, and firm texture complement the richness of duck, be it wild or domestic.

Autumn is the best season for leeks and Jerusalem artichokes. The latter may be hard to find, but the flavour is worth pursuing.

Braised Leeks

12 small to medium leeks
2 ½ cups lightly salted beef
   stock (see basic recipes)
¼ cup butter
2 tbsp finely chopped parsley

Remove the roots and cut the leeks off about 8" from the base. Slit the green part down to the white and wash very thoroughly under running cold water. Lay the leeks in a heat-proof dish that holds them comfortably in 2 layers. Pour on the stock, dot with butter, cover loosely with aluminum foil. Place on direct heat, bring to the boil, reduce the heat to medium, and simmer 30 minutes or until the leeks are tender and most of the liquid absorbed. Place in the oven to cook another 15-20 minutes. The leeks should be golden brown. Sprinkle with parsley and serve.

2 ducks, 4-5 lbs each
½ tsp salt
½ tsp freshly ground pepper
1 tsp salt

Giblet Stock:
giblets and necks
5 cups water
½ tsp salt
¼ tsp freshly ground pepper
1 bay leaf
¼ tsp dried crushed thyme or ½
  tsp chopped fresh thyme
½ stalk celery
1 small onion

Wild Rice Stuffing:
3 tbsp butter
½ cup finely chopped onions
6 cups sliced mushrooms
¼ cup finely chopped celery
1 ½ cups wild rice
3 cups hot giblet stock
½ tsp dried crushed sage or 1
  tsp chopped fresh sage
½ tsp dried crushed thyme or 1
  tsp chopped fresh thyme
3 tbsp chopped parsley
¼ tsp salt
¼ tsp freshly ground pepper
½ cup heavy cream

Duck with Wild Rice and Mushrooms

Wipe ducks with a damp cloth, pat dry, prick the skin with a fork, and sprinkle the cavities with the ½ tsp salt and pepper.

Place ducks breast down on a rack in a shallow open roasting pan large enough to accommodate them comfortably. Roast at 350 degrees about 25-30 minutes per pound. After 45 minutes, turn the ducks breast up, prick again, and continue cooking. Periodically remove excess fat from the pan. The ducks are cooked when the skin is crisp and a drumstick moves easily. Remove from the rack to a preheated platter. Sprinkle with the 1 tsp salt and set in a warm place. Drain the fat from the roasting pan, leaving the brown drippings.

As soon as the ducks are in the oven, rinse the giblets and necks. Place them in a saucepan with the water, the ½ tsp salt, ¼ tsp freshly ground pepper, bay leaf, the ¼ tsp thyme, ½ stalk celery, and the small onion. Bring to the boil, skim carefully, reduce heat, and simmer 1 ½ hours or until the giblets are tender and the stock somewhat reduced. Strain the stock, keep warm.

1 hour before serving time, melt the butter in a heavy-bottomed saucepan. Add the chopped onions, mushrooms, and celery. Stir to coat the vegetables. Cook 2-3 minutes. Add the rice, stir again, and cook 3-4 minutes more. Add the hot stock, the remaining herbs, salt, and pepper. Mix together. Bring to the boil, reduce heat, cover, and bake in the oven 30 minutes or until the rice is tender but not mushy and the stock is absorbed.

When the ducks are ready, stir the heavy cream into the drippings in the roasting pan. Place over medium heat, stirring and scraping the particles off the pan. Pour this sauce over the rice, and gently mix it in with a fork. Taste, add more salt if desired.

To serve, run a small sharp knife along the middle of the breastbone of the duck, then carefully cut under the breast meat on each side. Snip out the rib cage, using poultry shears. Spread the 2 sides apart gently. Spoon the stuffing into the cavity, heaping it up lavishly. Garnish the platter with plenty of parsley.

Alternately, spoon a bed of the rice dressing around the duck in the platter.

2 lbs Jerusalem artichokes
½ tsp salt
boiling water

Sauce:
1 tbsp butter
1 tbsp flour
½ cup milk
½ cup artichoke water
½ tsp salt
¼ tsp freshly ground pepper
1 tbsp grated cheddar cheese
2 tbsp crisp bread crumbs

Creamed Jerusalem Artichokes

Peel the artichokes carefully, dividing into pieces according to the nobs.

Place the artichokes and the first ½ tsp salt in a saucepan, cover with boiling water. Cover, bring to the boil, reduce heat, and simmer 10-15 minutes or until tender. Drain, reserving ½ cup of the cooking liquid.

Place the artichokes in a greased, shallow, ovenproof dish. Cover and keep warm.

Melt the butter, add the flour, and cook 2-3 minutes over medium heat. Gradually add the milk and artichoke water, stirring well to prevent lumps. Add the second ½ tsp salt, pepper, and cheese. Reduce heat to low, cook 5 minutes. Pour the sauce over the artichokes, covering them evenly. Sprinkle on the crumbs and brown under the grill 2-3 minutes.

---

1 head curly endive
1 stalk tender, inner celery
½ green pepper

Dressing:
1 ½ tbsp wine vinegar
6 tbsp oil
1 tsp salt
¼ tsp freshly ground pepper
¼ tsp dry mustard
½ tsp crushed dried tarragon or
    1 tsp chopped fresh tarragon

Green Pepper and Endive Salad

Remove the bitter outer leaves of an endive. Tear the tender leaves into bite-sized pieces. Cut the celery into thin diagonal slices. Cut the green pepper into thin lengthwise slices. Place the endive in a bowl. Arrange the celery in the middle and the green peppers around the edge. Combine the dressing ingredients. Just before serving, pour over the vegetables, bring to the table, and toss lightly.

½ cup sifted cake flour
¼ cup cocoa
¾ tsp baking powder
¼ tsp salt
4 eggs, separated
¾ cup white sugar
1 drop red food colouring
1 tsp vanilla
¼ cup icing sugar

Topping:
½ pint heavy cream
1 tsp white sugar
2-3 drops almond extract
½ cup sliced almonds, toasted
   if desired (see basic recipes)

Chocolate Almond Sponge Roll

Grease a 10″ x 5″ x 1″ jelly roll pan. Cut a piece of waxed paper to fit the bottom. Grease the paper well.

Sift together the flour, cocoa, baking powder, and salt.

Beat egg yolks until thick. Continue beating, gradually adding the white sugar. The mixture should become thick and light yellow-coloured.

Add the sifted dry ingredients to the yolks. Combine well.

Add the food colouring and vanilla to this batter.

Beat the egg whites until stiff but not dry. Fold them very carefully into the batter.

Bake 13 minutes at 375 degrees. In the meantime, sprinkle a small tea towel with icing sugar.

Remove from the oven, loosen edges of cake with a knife. Turn the pan over on the sugary towel. Gently pull off the pan and the waxed paper, using the towel as a help. Roll up the cake lengthwise and cool the cake rolled up on a rack.

Whip the cream. Add the 1 tsp sugar and almond extract. Spread over the cooled chocolate roll. Sprinkle with almonds.

Apple Extravaganza

Cider Baked Sauerkraut
with
Pickled or Smoked Pork Loin
and
Farmer's Sausage
Caraway Seed Potatoes with Sour Cream
Dilled Bean Sticks and Dill Pickles

Choice of:
Schnitz Apple Pie
Lumber Camp Apple Pie
Pippin Apple Sauce Pie
Dutch Apple Cake
Dried Apple Cake
Apple Dumplings Supreme
Apple Fritters
Baked Apples with Rum and Cider Sauce

Apples abound from coast to coast, but Nova Scotia, Quebec, Ontario, and British Columbia are the major producing provinces. The range of varieties is enormous, and every kind of apple is worth exploring for cooking or eating. There is a supply of apples in prime ripeness from the end of July (Yellow Transparent) to late November (Northern Spy, Golden Russet), and the 20-odd varieties marketed commercially do not include many old-fashioned favourites still found in some orchards and fondly remembered by older generations: Red Astrakhan, Pippin, Baldwin, King, St. Lawrence, and Tolman Sweet.

Apples became the Canadian fruit because they were easy to store and could therefore extend the fresh fruit season. They also form the basis of innumerable chutneys, pickles, jellies, and sauces. Drying, once a very common method of preserving apples as well as numerous other fruits in Canada, lengthened their season even more. This old art is still practised by descendents of the Pennsylvania Dutch and figures in many of their specialties. Schnitzing, or cutting up, apples for drying gave schnitz apple pie its name. Dried apples have been used in an enormous variety of pies, cakes, puddings, and compotes.

Apple butter is a unique Canadian product. It is basically apple sauce (preferably made from Tolman Sweets and Snow Apples) boiled down with cider to a thick, rich brown sauce. Its tart flavour is wonderful on bread, toast, biscuits, or muffins.

From the enormous range of apple desserts, eight of the best have been included here.

For recipes for dilled bean sticks and dill pickles, see the preserves section at the end of the book.

---

10 slices of bacon
1 cup finely chopped onions
1 ½ cups cored sliced apples
3 lbs fresh sauerkraut (6 cups)
1 clove garlic, minced
½ tsp freshly ground pepper
6 juniper berries
6 cups cider or beer
one 4-lb loin of pork, fresh,
    pickled, or smoked
1 ½-lb piece of farmer's sausage

Cider Baked Sauerkraut with Pickled or Smoked Loin of Pork and Farmer's Sausage

Line a large ovenproof dish with bacon slices. Add half the onions and apples. Rinse the sauerkraut under cold running water. Drain well. Place half the sauerkraut in the dish. Add the garlic, pepper, juniper berries, the rest of the onions and apples, and finally the remaining sauerkraut. Pour in the cider. Cover and cook at 300 degrees 4-5 hours.

2 ½ hours before the end of the cooking time, add the loin of pork, pushing it down somewhat into the sauerkraut. 45 minutes before the end of the cooking time, add the farmer's sausage, pushing it down as well. 10 minutes before the end of the cooking time, lift up the meat, turn on the grill, and cook the meat until brown and crisp.

To serve, heap the sauerkraut onto a big preheated platter. Slice the loin of pork, cut the sausages into 3" pieces, and arrange around the sauerkraut.

---

6 medium potatoes
boiling water
1 tsp salt
3 tbsp butter
2 tsp caraway seeds
¾ cup sour cream

Caraway Seed Potatoes with Sour Cream

Peel the potatoes. Drop into boiling water to cover and add the salt. Cover, bring to the boil, reduce heat, and boil gently 20 to 25 minutes or until tender. Drain. Shake dry over heat. Add the butter and caraway seed, turning the potatoes to coat evenly. Place in a preheated serving dish and pass with the sour cream.

Schnitz Apple Pie

one 10″ unbaked, unpricked
  pie shell (see basic recipes)
4 large or 6 medium cooking
  apples (for example, Yellow
  Transparents in August,
  Wealthies and Duchess in
  September, Courtlands in
  October, Greenings and Spies
  in November)
¼ cup thick cream, sweet or
  freshly soured
¾ cup firmly packed brown
  sugar
¼ cup butter
2 tbsp flour
1 tsp ground cinnamon

Cut each apple into 6 pieces. Peel and core each section. Arrange attractively in 1 layer in the pie shell.

Sprinkle on the cream, followed by the brown sugar, the butter cut in little pieces, the flour, and the cinnamon.

Bake 15 minutes at 450 degrees. Reduce heat to 350 degrees and continue baking 30-40 minutes or until the apples are tender and the crust is nicely browned.

Lumber Camp Apple Pie

9″ pie plate
1 tsp butter
5-6 tart cooking apples, peeled,
  cored, and sliced
⅔ cup firmly packed brown
  sugar
⅛ tsp salt
1 tbsp cornstarch
¼ tsp freshly grated nutmeg
1 tbsp butter
sufficient pie crust for top of
  pie (see basic recipes)
¾ cup whipping cream
1 tsp sugar
¼ tsp vanilla or rose water

Butter the pie plate generously with the 1 tsp butter. Fill evenly with apple slices to a level slightly higher than the rim.

Combine brown sugar, salt, cornstarch, and nutmeg. Sprinkle over the apples, probe gently to distribute through the top layers of the apples. Dot with 1 tbsp butter.

Cover top of apples with a pie crust. Crimp the edges. Cut one small slash ¼″ long for steam to escape.

Bake at 450 degrees for 10 minutes. Reduce heat to 350 degrees and continue baking another 40-50 minutes or until the crust is golden brown and the apples are tender.

Cool. Loosen the crust around the edges. Place large flat serving plate over the pie and turn over. Lift off the pie plate carefully.

Whip cream, add sugar and flavouring. Spread decoratively all over the apples. Serve immediately.

Pippin Apple Sauce Pie

one 9″ unbaked, unpricked pie shell (see basic recipes)
1 orange, preferably a Seville orange
water
6 cups peeled, cored, and sliced apples (7-8 medium apples)
2 tbsp water
¾ cup white sugar
whipped cream or custard sauce (see basic recipes)

Pare the zest from the orange. Shred finely and boil till tender in enough water to cover, 10-15 minutes. Drain and reserve. Squeeze the juice from the orange.

Put the apples and 2 tbsp water in a heavy-bottomed saucepan with a close-fitting lid. Cook over medium-low heat until the apples are tender, about 30 minutes. Mash.

Add the sugar, orange zest, and juice. Continue cooking uncovered over medium-low heat until the sauce is thick and amber-coloured, about 10-15 minutes. Stir almost constantly. Cool.

Pour the thick apple sauce into the pie shell. Bake at 400 degrees for 30-35 minutes or until the crust is golden brown. Cool.

Serve garnished with whipped cream or with a pitcher of custard sauce.

Dutch Apple Cake

Batter:
1 cup sifted all-purpose flour
½ tsp salt
1 ½ tsp baking powder
3 tbsp sugar
¼ cup butter
1 egg
¼ cup milk

Topping:
4 cups sliced, peeled, and cored apples
3 tbsp white sugar
1 tsp ground cinnamon
¼ cup melted butter
½ cup currant jelly, melted (optional; see preserves section)

Sift together the flour, salt, baking powder, and sugar into a large bowl.

Work in the butter with a pastry blender until the mixture is crumbly.

Beat the egg and milk together and add them to the mixture, stirring with a fork to form a dough. Don't beat.

Spread this dough (it will be fairly wet) into a buttered 12″ x 8″ baking tin.

Arrange the fruit over the dough in overlapping rows.

Combine the sugar and cinnamon and sprinkle them over the fruit.

Pour the melted butter evenly over the top.

Bake at 400 degrees for 35 minutes. The fruit should be tender, the crust crispy. Cool.

Spread with melted jelly if desired.

This recipe is excellent when either plums or peaches are substituted for the apples.

1 cup dried apples, firmly
    packed down
1 ½ cups water
½ cup molasses or maple syrup
½ cup corn syrup
½ cup butter
1 cup firmly packed brown
    sugar
1 egg, well beaten
2 cups sifted pastry flour
½ tsp ground cassia or
    cinnamon
½ tsp ground allspice
¼ tsp freshly grated nutmeg
1 tsp soda
½ tsp salt
½ cup buttermilk

Icing:
½ cup sifted icing sugar
2-3 tsp boiling water
2 drops vanilla

Dried Apple Cake

Soak apples overnight in the 1 ½ cups water. By morning, the apples will have absorbed almost all the water. Add the molasses and corn syrup. Simmer one hour. The apples will be tender and moist, and the liquid will be almost all absorbed. Remove from heat. Add the butter. Stir till melted. Cool. Blend in the brown sugar and egg.

Sift together the flour, spices, soda, and salt. Add to the apple mixture in 3 parts alternately with the buttermilk in 2 parts. Begin and end with the dry ingredients.

Pour into a well-greased 9" x 5" loaf tin. Bake at 325 degrees for 60-70 minutes or until a skewer inserted in the middle comes out clean.

Cool 10 minutes. Turn out onto a rack. Cool.

Place the icing sugar in a small bowl. Add enough boiling water to dissolve the icing sugar. Add vanilla and pour over cake, allowing it to drip decoratively over the edge. Serve in ½" slices.

A moist, spicy cake.

---

3 cups white sugar
1 cup sweet cider or water
6 cups peeled, cored, quartered
    tart cooking apples (5 large
    apples)
⅓ cup butter
⅓ cup white sugar
1 egg
1 tsp vanilla
2 ¼ cups sifted all-purpose
    flour
2 tbsp baking powder
¾ tsp salt
1 ⅛ cups milk or light cream
1 ½ tsp ground cinnamon

Apple Dumplings Supreme

Combine the 3 cups sugar and cider in a heavy-bottomed saucepan. Bring to the boil. Add the apples. Return to the boil. Reduce heat and simmer until the apples are transparent but not broken up, about 25 minutes.

In the meantime, cream the butter till light and fluffy. Gradually beat in the ⅓ cup sugar. Add the egg. Beat well. Stir in the vanilla. Sift together the flour, baking powder, and salt. Add the dry ingredients in 3 parts alternately with the milk in 2 parts to the creamed mixture. Begin and end with the dry ingredients.

Spoon the batter and apples plus syrup alternately into a well-greased 9" x 14" baking dish. Pour over any remaining syrup. Sprinkle with cinnamon.

Bake at 450 degrees for 10 minutes. Reduce heat to 400 and bake for 15-20 minutes or until, according to the personal recipe book of Hugh Forbes, "it is baked with crisp brown bits of paste risen here and there and through little rivers of syrup it will be crisp and soft, solid, liquid, jellied, spicy, bland and apply all through."

Apple Fritters

1 cup all-purpose flour
1 ½ tsp baking powder
½ tsp salt
2 tbsp white sugar
1 egg, well beaten
½ cup plus 2 tbsp milk
¼ tsp grated lemon rind
1 ½ cups sweet apples, peeled, cored, and chopped

Cinnamon Coating:
½ cup sugar
2 tbsp ground cinnamon

Sift dry ingredients together into a large bowl.

Add well-beaten egg and milk and grated lemon rind. Stir well until batter is smooth. Add apples.

Drop by spoonfuls into deep fat at 375 degrees. Fry 2 minutes on each side or until puffed up and golden brown. Drain on a paper towel. Combine the ½ cup sugar and cinnamon in a paper bag and shake the fritters gently in this mixture. Makes 12-15 fritters.

Baked Apples with Rum and Cider Sauce

6 large apples (Northern Spies are excellent for this recipe)
2 tbsp raisins
24 whole blanched almonds
9 tbsp brown sugar
2 tbsp butter
⅓ cup water
1 tbsp rum
1 cup sweet cider
1 tbsp cornstarch
¼ tsp freshly grated nutmeg
whipped cream (see basic recipes)

Wash and core apples, leaving about ½" of apple at the bottom to hold the filling. In each apple place 1 tsp raisins, 4 whole almonds, 1 ½ tbsp brown sugar and 1 tsp butter. Score the skin at the top of the apple into sixths. As the apple cooks, it will open like a flower and not split unattractively.

Place the apples in an open, ovenproof dish big enough to accommodate them without touching. Combine the water and rum and pour in. Bake at 375 degrees until the apples are tender, about 30-50 minutes depending upon the variety (McIntosh take about 30, a firm variety like Northern Spies up to 50 minutes). Baste periodically with the pan juices. Remove the apples to a warm platter.

Shake the cider and cornstarch together in a jar. Combine with the pan juices (in a saucepan if the baking dish does not go on the top of the stove). Cook until thick and clear. Stir in the nutmeg.

Pour some sauce over each apple. Serve the rest in a jug. Pass light cream or whipped heavy cream if desired.

Grilled Steak with Oyster Stuffing Dinner

Classic Cream of Tomato Soup
or
Clear Tomato Bouillon with Croutons

Grilled Steaks with Oyster Stuffing
Buttered Parsnips with Nutmeg

Marinated Red Cabbage Salad

Baked Indian Pudding

Suggested wine:
full-bodied red

We know that some nineteenth-century Canadians grew tomatoes solely for decoration, believing the fruit to be poisonous. Nevertheless, tomato recipes can be found in the first cookbooks published in Canada. Tomato dishes have changed and multiplied over the years, but one that has easily retained its popularity is cream of tomato soup. This soup was made annually in a condensed form and stored in quart sealers for the winter; the recipe usually called for tomatoes by the peck! The second, less familiar tomato soup originates in the 1914 *Canadian Family Cook Book*. It is beautifully clear, thanks to the egg whites, and has a slight savour of cloves.

The pudding recipe is a bare nod to the veritable gold mine of Canadian puddings. All early cookbooks—whether published or hand-written personal collections—contain a large number of steamed and baked puddings with names like Paradise, Surprise, Bachelors, Eve's, Duke of Cumberland, and Speckled Jim. There is a basic preparation for the steamed puddings of bread crumbs, suet, eggs, and milk, supplemented by dried or fresh fruits, jams or marmalades, liquor, and usually lots of spices. Pudding sauces varied too. Custard was a favourite; so were potent wine or sherry sauces and hard sauces made with brown sugar, orange, rum, lemon, or caramel. Thick fresh cream and maple syrup are unbeatable simple sauces. Butter has replaced suet in these puddings, because it shortens the steaming time drastically and because the results with butter are as good if not better than with suet.

¼ cup butter
½ cup chopped onion (1 medium)
¾ cup chopped carrots (2 medium)
¾ cup chopped celery (1 stalk)
2 ½ lbs ripe red tomatoes (8 medium), quartered
¼ cup flour
1 cup lightly salted chicken stock (see basic recipes)
4 stalks parsley
1 bay leaf
2 whole cloves
⅛ tsp cayenne pepper
1 tbsp white sugar
1 ½ tsp salt
1 cup light cream
1 cup milk

Garnish:
croutons (see recipe for Clear Tomato Bouillon)
or
½ cup whipped cream
pinch salt
1 tbsp finely chopped parsley
1 tsp finely chopped chives

Classic Cream of Tomato Soup

Melt the butter in a large, heavy-bottomed saucepan. Add the onion, carrots, and celery. Stir to coat the vegetables. Cover and cook over a low heat 3-4 minutes.

Add the tomatoes. Stir. Cover and cook over a low heat 3-4 minutes. Stir in flour, continue to cook and stir 3-4 minutes more. Add the stock gradually, stirring all the time, and then add the parsley, bay leaf, cloves, cayenne pepper, sugar, and salt. Simmer uncovered 30-40 minutes or until all the vegetables are tender and the soup is thick and smooth.

Pass the soup through a sieve or food mill. Taste. Add more salt or sugar if needed.

Just before serving, heat the soup through. Scald the cream and milk and add to the soup. Serve with croutons (see below) or a dollop of lightly salted whipped cream and finely chopped parsley and chives.

Soup:
3 ½ cups stewed or canned
   tomatoes
5 cups lightly salted beef stock
   (see basic recipes)
¼ cup finely chopped onions
2 bay leaves
3 whole cloves
½ tsp freshly ground pepper
1 teaspoon celery seed
3 egg whites
salt
2 tbsp dry sherry

Croutons:
¼ cup butter
2 slices homemade white or
   stone-ground brown bread
   (see basic recipes)
¼ tsp salt

Clear Tomato Bouillon with Croutons

Combine all the ingredients for the soup except the egg whites, salt, and sherry. Cover, bring to the boil, reduce heat, and simmer 20 minutes. Strain.

Return the strained soup to a clean saucepan. Beat egg whites until frothy. Add to the soup and return to the boil. Boil 6 minutes, strain through two thicknesses of rinsed cheesecloth. Reheat. Taste. Add salt if necessary, and sherry.

Melt the butter in a frying pan over medium-low heat. Cube the bread. Fry it until it is golden brown on all sides. Drain on paper towel and sprinkle lightly with salt.

Serve the soup in bowls. Pass croutons separately.

6 strip steaks 1 ¼"-1 ½" thick
   (strip steaks are the boneless
   steaks opposite the fillet on a
   T-bone or porterhouse steak)
4 oz cooked canned oysters,
   drained and chopped
   coarsely *or*
½ pint fresh shucked oysters
6 tbsp fresh fine bread crumbs
3 tbsp melted butter
3 tbsp finely chopped green
   onions or chives
1 tbsp finely chopped parsley
3 tbsp lemon juice
½ tsp salt
¼ tsp freshly ground pepper
oil
salt
freshly ground pepper

Grilled Steaks with Oyster Stuffing

If using fresh oysters, drain and sauté gently until tender in 2 tbsp butter (about 10 minutes).

Slit a 4" pocket in the side of each steak. Using a sharp knife, extend the pocket far enough into the steak for stuffing.

Combine the oysters, crumbs, butter, onions, parsley, lemon juice, ½ tsp salt, and ¼ tsp pepper and stuff each steak with one-sixth of the dressing. Close the pockets by sewing or using poultry pins, small skewers, or toothpicks.

Rub the outside of the steaks gently with oil. Grind pepper over each side.

Broil 8-10 minutes per side 4" from the source of heat. Salt lightly. Serve.

12 small or 8 medium parsnips
3 cups hot, lightly salted chicken stock (see basic recipes)
¼ tsp salt
2 tbsp butter, melted
⅛ tsp freshly grated nutmeg

Buttered Parsnips with Nutmeg

Peel but do not cut the parsnips. Place in a saucepan, add the stock and salt, cover, bring to the boil, reduce heat, and simmer about 15 minutes or until tender but not mushy. Drain the stock, reserving for another use. Pour over the butter, sprinkle on the nutmeg and shake the pan to coat all sides of the parsnips. Serve with the parsnips arranged parallel to each other.

4 cups finely shredded red cabbage
1 large onion, peeled and sliced thinly
¼ cup white sugar
½ tsp salt
¼ cup white wine vinegar
½ tsp dry mustard
2 tbsp white sugar
1 ½ tsp celery seed
¼ cup oil

Marinated Red Cabbage Salad

Place the cabbage, onion slices, ¼ cup sugar, and salt in a large bowl.

Combine the vinegar, mustard, 2 tbsp sugar, and celery seed in a saucepan. Bring to the boil. Add oil. Return to the boil. Remove from heat and pour immediately over the cabbage mixture. Mix thoroughly. Chill overnight.

Drain well before serving.

Will keep 2 weeks.

2 cups milk
5 tbsp cornmeal
2 cups light cream
½ cup molasses
1 tsp salt
¾ tsp ground allspice
½ tsp ground ginger
½ tsp ground cinnamon
¼ tsp freshly grated nutmeg
2 eggs, well beaten
¾ cup firmly packed brown sugar
2 tbsp butter, melted
1 cup cold milk

Baked Indian Pudding

Scald the milk in the top of a double boiler over direct heat. Stir in the cornmeal and cook 5 minutes, stirring constantly until the mixture is smooth and begins to thicken. Cover and cook over boiling water 25 minutes. Cool slightly. Add the cream, molasses, salt, spices, eggs, brown sugar, and butter. Pour into a greased, 2-quart, ovenproof dish. Bake at 300 degrees for 30 minutes. Pour the cold milk over the pudding. Continue baking 2 more hours at 300 degrees. Serve warm with a jug of heavy cream.

Victorian Jugged or Roasted Rabbit Dinner

Corn Chowder

Jugged Hare with Forcemeat Balls
or
Roasted Rabbit with Relishing Stuffing
Sweet and Sour Red Cabbage with Apples

Endive and Lettuce Salad with Pepper Dressing

Seeded Malaga Raisin Pie

Suggested wine:
dry red or chilled rosé

How Mrs. Beeton got around! This recipe for jugged hare is an adaptation of one found in a 1900 Brantford, Ontario, cookbook. Later, however, I traced it back to Mrs. Beeton's *Modern Household Cookery*, published in 1861. The forcemeat balls are part of the original garnish. They are not to be done without, for they provide a crisp texture and contrasting taste to the rabbit.

Wild hare has become known in Canada by the general term rabbit. If wild is unavailable, the domestic variety substitutes well as long as the cooking time is reduced accordingly.

The roast rabbit is from the *Manual of Cookery*. The original recipe calls for a "large relishing stuffing" in the "belly" and says the ears "must be nicely cleaned and singed. They are reckoned a dainty." Use the ingredients for the forcemeat balls to make the relishing stuffing and forget the ears. Big bunches of parsley at that end of the platter will substitute nicely.

Many Canadians, especially those living in the North, are still able to enjoy a full repertoire of game. For those who can't, rabbit is one elegant way to share this heritage. Until recently rabbit was the one game animal available for sale, but the drastic reduction in rabbits due to commercial hunting brought an abrupt end to this.

6 slices of lean bacon
½ cup sliced onions
½ cup chopped celery
1 tbsp flour
¾ tsp salt
¼ tsp freshly ground pepper
2 cups hot chicken stock (see
   basic recipes) or boiling
   water
3 cups finely diced potatoes
1 ½ cups fresh or canned corn
   kernels
2 ½-3 cups milk

Corn Chowder

Chop bacon, sauté 4-5 minutes in a large heavy-bottomed stock pot or saucepan. Add onions and celery and cook over a low heat until transparent, about 5 minutes.

Stir in the flour, salt, and pepper. Cook 3-4 minutes.

Gradually blend in the hot stock, then add the potatoes. Cover. Simmer 10 minutes. Add corn. Simmer 10 more minutes. The vegetables should all be tender but not mushy. Scald the milk and add to the soup to the desired consistency.

Serve with crackers. Enough for 8-10.

1 rabbit, 2 ½-3 lbs
3 tbsp flour
¼ cup butter
4 quarts boiling water
3 cups beef stock (see basic
    recipes)
2 medium onions
6 whole cloves
1 lemon, peeled and cut in half
½ tsp freshly ground pepper
⅛ tsp cayenne pepper
2 sprigs fresh marjoram (can
    use summer savory or thyme)
    or ½ tsp crushed dried herbs
salt
2 tbsp flour
2 tbsp butter
¼ cup port wine
1 tbsp finely chopped chives
2 tbsp finely chopped parsley

Victorian Jugged Hare with Forcemeat Balls

Cut the rabbit into 12 pieces. Pat dry with a cloth. Shake each piece in a bag with the 3 tbsp flour. Melt the ¼ cup butter and brown the rabbit pieces on all sides over medium heat.

Prepare the cooking containers. You will need a large pot, a rack to fit the bottom of it, and a smaller heatproof container that is large enough to contain the rabbit (2-3 quarts) and that will fit into the larger container. Begin by pouring 2 quarts of boiling water into the larger pot. Put over medium heat. Cover. Have another 2 quarts of water boiling.

Put the rabbit into the smaller pot. Pour the stock into the pan where the rabbit browned. Heat, work off all the particles with a wooden spoon. Remove from the heat. Reserve.

Stick the cloves into the onions. Add to the rabbit along with the two peeled lemon halves, pepper, cayenne pepper, and marjoram. Pour in the stock and add salt only if the stock is unsalted.

Cover the smaller pot with aluminum foil, press closely around the edge, and tie up tightly with string. Place on the rack and immerse into the boiling water in the larger container. Add more boiling water, until it reaches 1" from the top of the smaller pot when the water is boiling. Cover. Boil gently 2 hours for young domestic rabbit, 3-4 hours for older wild varieties. The meat should be very tender. Replenish boiling water as it evaporates.

Remove smaller pot. Uncover. Place rabbit pieces in a preheated serving dish, cover lightly, and place in a warm oven. Strain the cooking liquid, reduce by ¼ over high heat, work the 2 tbsp flour and 2 tbsp butter together, and gradually add this to thicken the stock. Add the port, correct seasoning, and pour over the rabbit pieces. Sprinkle with chives and parsley. Garnish with forcemeat balls (see below).

Note: this recipe serves 4-5.

1 ½ cups fine bread crumbs
  from stale but not dry
  homemade bread (see basic
  recipes)
¼ cup finely chopped ham or
  lean bacon
¼ cup melted butter
grated rind of ½ lemon
1 tsp minced parsley
1 tsp minced fresh summer
  savory or thyme or ½ tsp
  dried crushed
¼ tsp salt
few grains of cayenne pepper
¼ tsp ground mace
2 eggs, lightly beaten
1 quart oil or 2 ½ lbs shortening
  or lard

Forcemeat Balls or Relishing Stuffing

Combine all the ingredients except the fat for frying. Work well together with the hands. Form into 16 compact balls.

Heat the oil, shortening or lard slowly to 365 degrees in a 3-quart saucepan. (The fat can be reused if you strain it through cheesecloth, pour into a clean jar and keep it in a cool place until needed.) Fry the forcemeat balls, 3-4 at a time, until golden brown, about 2-3 minutes. Turn once during the cooking time. Drain on paper towel. Garnish jugged hare.

For stuffing, combine all the ingredients except the fat. Do not form into balls.

---

1 rabbit, 2-3 pounds
¼" slice of lemon
¼ cup melted butter
½ tsp finely crushed dried
  summer savory or 1 tsp
  chopped fresh summer
  savory
½ tsp freshly ground pepper
1 tsp flour
salt (about 1 tsp)
stuffing (see forcemeat recipe
  above)
parsley

Roasted Rabbit with Relishing Stuffing

Remove head. Dry rabbit. Wipe rabbit all over with lemon slice, pressing the juice out as you do so. Fill the cavity with the loose forcemeat stuffing. Skewer shut. Lay on a rack in an open roasting pan. Leave a few minutes to dry.

Brush one side with melted butter and sprinkle on half the summer savory and half the pepper. Turn the rabbit on the other side and repeat, reserving as much of the butter as remains for basting the rabbit. Roast at 350 degrees for 30 minutes per pound, basting frequently, first with the rest of the melted butter and then with the accumulated pan juices.

Halfway through the cooking time, turn the rabbit onto its other side and continue roasting and basting. 10 minutes before the end of the calculated roasting time, sprinkle the flour evenly over the rabbit. Return to the oven. Baste twice more to set the crust to a nice crisp golden brown.

Remove from the oven, salt both sides. Place on a preheated platter and garnish lavishly with parsley.

Note: this recipe serves 4-5.

3 tbsp bacon drippings or
    butter
⅓ cup finely chopped onions
9 cups shredded red cabbage
    (1 medium head)
1 cup cored, diced tart apples
3 tbsp cider vinegar
3 tbsp brown sugar
1 tbsp caraway seeds
1 tsp salt
¼ tsp freshly ground pepper
⅓ cup raisins

Sweet and Sour Red Cabbage with Apples

Melt drippings or butter in a large, heavy-bottomed saucepan. Sauté the onion lightly in the fat, about 5 minutes. Add the cabbage. Stir well to coat the cabbage, cover, and continue cooking over moderate heat for 5 minutes. Add remaining ingredients. Stir well. Cover and cook about another 10 minutes until the cabbage is tender but not mushy.

½ medium head of endive
½ small head of lettuce,
    preferably romaine
1 green onion, finely chopped
4-5 mushrooms, sliced

Dressing:
¾-1 tsp freshly ground black
    pepper
½ tsp salt
¼ tsp dry mustard
¼ cup oil
1 ½ tbsp white wine vinegar

Endive and Lettuce Salad with Pepper Dressing

Break the endive and lettuce into bite-sized pieces (there should be about 4 cups of each). Sprinkle with the onion and mushrooms.

Combine the rest of the ingredients in a small bowl. Just before serving, pour the dressing over the greens and toss lightly to coat every leaf. Try the dressing with the ¾ tsp of pepper. If the salad is not peppery enough, add the full quantity.

sufficient pastry for a 2-crust,
    10″ pie (see basic recipes)
2 cups seeded raisins
2 cups boiling water
1 tsp grated orange rind
¼ tsp salt
1 cup firmly packed brown
    sugar
3 tbsp cornstarch
⅓ cup orange juice
1 tbsp lemon juice
1 tbsp butter

Seeded Malaga Raisin Pie

Simmer raisins, boiling water, orange rind, and salt for 10 minutes in a covered saucepan.

Thoroughly combine brown sugar and cornstarch. Gradually add to the raisin mixture, stirring to prevent lumps. Cook over medium heat until the sauce is thick and clear. There should be no taste of raw cornstarch.

Remove from the heat. Add orange juice, lemon juice, and butter. Cool.

Line a 10″ pie plate with pastry. Do not trim. Add cooked raisin mixture. Moisten pastry around the edge of the pie plate. Cover with top pastry, trim, flute. Cut a few decorative slashes in the top.

Bake at 450 degrees for 15 minutes, reduce heat to 350, and continue baking 20 to 25 minutes more or until the pastry is beautifully browned.

Roast Capon with Potato and Crouton Stuffing Dinner

Pumpkin Soup

Roast Capon with Potato and Crouton Stuffing
Grilled Tomatoes with Basil

Lemon and Bacon Spinach Salad

Plum Pie

Suggested wine:
chilled white, chilled rosé, or dry red

I know soup is an unexpected pumpkin recipe. Pumpkin is usually associated with pies and, to a lesser extent, muffins, marmalade, tea breads, and cookies. Recently, however, this fruit-vegetable has been enjoying a minor revival and appearing in many unexpected places—chiffon pies, fine cakes, bavarian creams, and ice cream, to name a few. The soup recipe in this menu appeared in the *Canadian Cook Book* in 1908. Squash substitutes well for pumpkin recipes as long as the consistency is the same.

Canadians eat a lot of poultry every year, about 35 pounds per person on the average. Of this approximately 23 pounds are chicken. For roasting, nothing is better than a capon, which is a desexed rooster raised exclusively for eating. Capons range from four to eight pounds, are well-fleshed, and have a lot of flavour. The mashed potato and crouton stuffing, Mennonite in origin, is well seasoned with sage and good enough to eat on its own.

one 2 ½-lb pumpkin or squash
   (7 cups when cut in 1" cubes)
¼ cup butter
1 cup chopped onions (2
   medium)
2 cups lightly salted chicken
   stock (see basic recipes)
1 tsp salt
½ tsp freshly ground pepper
2-2 ½ cups light cream
½ cup finely chopped ham
   (optional)

Croutons:
4 tbsp butter
2 slices homemade white
   bread (see basic recipes)
⅛ tsp mace
nutmeg

Pumpkin Soup

Peel the pumpkin or squash and dice into 1" cubes. Melt the butter in a large, heavy-bottomed saucepan. Add the pumpkin and onions. Stir to coat. Cover and cook over low heat for 20 minutes.

Add the stock, salt, and pepper. Cover and simmer 15-20 minutes or until the pumpkin is tender. If using squash, blend the soup till smooth. Otherwise, pass the soup through a sieve or food mill to remove any fibers. Return to the saucepan. Add the cream to the desired consistency. Taste, add more salt if necessary. Heat through, but do not boil. Stir in the chopped ham.

Melt the butter for the croutons. Cut the bread into very small squares and fry gently until golden brown. Drain on paper towel. Sprinkle on mace.

Serve the soup in a tureen or bowls with croutons on top. Grate a little fresh nutmeg over the soup.

one 5-lb capon or roasting
   chicken
¼ lemon
½ tsp salt

Roast Capon with Potato and Crouton Stuffing

Wipe inside cavity with a damp cloth. Rub with lemon. Sprinkle inside lightly with ½ tsp salt. Fill neck and interior cavities lightly with stuffing (see below). Skewer openings. Truss. Make a paste of the 2 tbsp soft butter, mustard, and pepper. Lay the chicken breast side up in an open roasting pan. Spread the paste over it. Roast at 325 degrees about 35 minutes per pound or until a thermometer inserted in the thigh registers 190 degrees. Baste periodically, initially using the 1-2 tbsp melted butter and then accumulated pan juices. Remove to a preheated platter in a warm place.

Let stand 10 minutes before carving to set the flesh. This allows the juices to flow back into the tissues of the chicken, and makes it easier to carve.

Stuffing:
4 medium-large potatoes
boiling water
½ tsp salt
¼ cup butter
1 cup ½" bread cubes
¼ cup finely chopped onions
1 clove garlic, chopped fine
1 chicken liver, cut in 4
1 tsp dried crushed thyme or 2
   tsp chopped fresh thyme
2 tbsp finely chopped parsley
½ tsp freshly ground pepper
salt

Coating:
2 tbsp soft butter
2 tsp dry mustard
½ tsp freshly ground pepper

Basting:
1-2 tbsp melted butter

Potato and Crouton Stuffing:
Cut potatoes into quarters. Drop into boiling water, add salt, cover, and boil over moderate heat until tender, about 15-20 minutes. Drain, shake dry over heat and mash. Reserve 1 ½ cups potato water for gravy.

Melt 2 tbsp of the butter. Sauté the bread cubes in it until crisp and golden. Remove and reserve. Melt the rest of the butter for the stuffing. Add the onions, garlic, and liver. Cook until the onions are just transparent and the liver is firm. Chop the liver into small pieces. Combine onions, garlic, and liver with the bread cubes and 4 cups of the mashed potatoes. Add the herbs and pepper. Taste, add salt if necessary.

---

drippings
2 tbsp flour
1 ½ cups potato water
¼ tsp dry mustard
¼ tsp freshly grated pepper
salt

Pan Gravy

Skim fat from pan and stir flour into drippings with a wooden spoon to make a smooth paste. Place over medium heat. Add potato water gradually and the mustard and pepper. Stir until the gravy is smooth. Taste. Add salt if desired. Serve hot in a preheated gravy boat.

---

12 small tomatoes or 24 cherry
   tomatoes
2 tbsp butter, melted
1 tbsp oil
¾ tsp salt
¼ tsp freshly ground pepper
1 tsp finely chopped chives
½ tsp chopped fresh basil or ¼
   tsp dried crushed basil
1 tbsp finely chopped parsley

Grilled Tomatoes with Basil

Using a sharp pointed knife, trim out the stems of the tomatoes neatly.

Place the butter, oil, salt, and pepper in a shallow, ovenproof dish that will accommodate the tomatoes comfortably. Using a brush, coat each of the tomatoes with the butter and oil and turn stem end down in the dish.

Bake at 400 degrees for 10 minutes or until the skins just begin to break a little. Baste once with any accumulated juices. Sprinkle with the herbs and serve immediately.

Lemon and Bacon Spinach Salad

6 slices of bacon
1 lb spinach
½ cup olive oil
2 tbsp lemon juice
1 clove garlic
¾ tsp salt
¼ tsp freshly ground pepper
½ tsp chopped fresh marjoram
　or summer savory or ¼ tsp
　dried crushed marjoram or
　summer savory
2 hard-boiled eggs (optional)

Fry the bacon over medium heat till crisp. Drain on paper towel. Crumble. Reserve.

Wash the spinach in several changes of cold water. Trim off the stems and hard ribs. Roll in a dry tea towel, place in a plastic bag, and crisp for an hour in the refrigerator.

Combine the oil and lemon juice. Mash the garlic with the salt and add with the pepper and marjoram to the oil and lemon juice. Reserve.

Grate or chop finely the eggs. Reserve.

Just before serving, place the spinach in a large salad bowl. Sprinkle the bacon and grated egg on top. Pour on the dressing. Toss up lightly to coat all the leaves. Serve immediately.

Plum Pie

one 9″ unbaked, unpricked pie
　shell (see basic recipes)
4 cups prune plums, pitted and
　halved
3 tbsp sour cream
1 tbsp Seville orange
　marmalade (see preserves
　section)
¾ cup white sugar
2 tbsp flour
¼ tsp freshly grated nutmeg
1 tbsp butter
whipped cream (see basic
　recipes)

Arrange plums skin side up in the pie shell. Dot with sour cream and marmalade.

Combine the sugar, flour, and nutmeg. With a pastry blender, cut the butter in until the mixture is crumbly. Sprinkle the sugar mixture evenly over the plums.

Bake at 425 degrees for 10 minutes. Reduce heat to 350 and bake for 30-40 minutes. The crust should be golden brown and the fruit tender. Serve with whipped cream.

The Edgar Nutmeg Grater

Fall Breakfast

Concord Grape Juice

Buckwheat Pancakes with Maple Syrup
Homemade Pork Sausage Patties

Graham Gems

Banana Muffins

Apple Butter and Pumpkin Marmalade

Coffee

Following the fall butchering, every farmer used to make his own sausage according to his own recipe. Salt, black pepper, and sage were the traditional seasonings, but it was not unusual to add cloves, mace, allspice, nutmeg, and cayenne pepper. The best sausages available now are still homemade, but by small local butchers. Farm markets such as those in Kitchener, Stratford, and Ottawa are well supplied by butchers who take great care in the preparation of their own sausages. You can spot a good sausage by its obvious meat content (no bread filler), speckles of spices, and real casing. For this breakfast, I'm suggesting that we stretch a little and make our own sausage from scratch and our own grape juice.

The buckwheat pancakes were described by an early British immigrant as "a national dainty" and the "favorite breakfast dish with old Canadian settlers." There were good reasons for growing lots of buckwheat: it is easy to cultivate; it can be sown late and harvested early; and it can be ploughed under to enrich the soil. The leavening agent in old-time buckwheat pancakes was always yeast. The batter could be mixed up the night before and left to rise overnight, ready for a quick breakfast.

First cousins to pancakes are muffins (gems is an old word for them). The rougher flours such as graham, whole wheat, cornmeal, and bran give them a marked texture.

For apple butter and pumpkin marmalade, see the preserves section at the end of the book.

Concord Grape Juice

5 cups washed and stemmed
  Concord grapes
2 cups hot water
1 cup white sugar

Combine grapes and water in a saucepan. Bring to the boil and simmer covered 30 minutes or until very tender and falling apart. Strain through a fine sieve.

Measure 4 cups of the juice into a saucepan. Bring to a boil. Add the sugar and return to the boil.

Pour into sterilized sealers. Seal. Yield: about 2 pints.

To serve, dilute half and half with cold water.

Buckwheat Pancakes

¾ cup buckwheat flour
¾ cup sifted all-purpose flour
1 tbsp baking powder
3 tbsp white sugar
¾ tsp salt
1 egg, lightly beaten
1 ½ cups milk
3 tbsp melted butter, cooled

Stir together the dry ingredients.

Combine the egg, milk, and melted butter. Add to the dry ingredients, mixing just long enough to incorporate the flour. Do not beat.

Pour onto a hot griddle or a frying pan, lightly greased. Turn when the bubbles break and the batter does not fill the holes. Cook on the other side until the pancakes even out. Yield: 12 medium pancakes.

Serve with maple syrup.

Homemade Pork Sausage Patties

2 lbs twice-ground pork, even
  mixture of lean and fat
1 tbsp dried crushed sage
¾ tsp freshly ground pepper
¾ tsp salt
⅛ tsp ground allspice
⅛ tsp ground cloves
pinch of cayenne pepper

Combine all ingredients. Mix well with hands. Shape into 12 patties and fry till brown on both sides (about 20 minutes). No fat is needed to start the sausages.

½ cup shortening
1 cup firmly packed brown
  sugar
1 egg
½ cup sifted all-purpose flour
½ tsp salt
½ tsp soda
1 tsp baking powder
1 ¼ cups graham flour
1 cup sour milk or buttermilk
¾ cup raisins

Graham Gems

Cream shortening until light and fluffy. Cream in brown sugar and beat in the egg.

Sift together the all-purpose flour, salt, soda, and baking powder. Stir together with the graham flour.

Add the dry ingredients in 3 parts alternately with the sour milk or buttermilk in 2 parts to the brown sugar mixture. Stir in the raisins.

Fill greased muffin tins ⅔ full. Bake at 400 degrees for 15 minutes. They should spring back when lightly touched and should have come away from the side of the pan. Yield: 12-14 gems.

Serve hot.

3 large ripe bananas
¾ cup white sugar or firmly
  packed brown sugar
1 egg
1 ½ cups sifted all-purpose
  flour
1 tsp soda
1 tsp baking powder
¾ tsp salt
⅓ cup melted butter, cooled

Banana Muffins

Preheat oven to 350 degrees.

In a large mixing bowl, put the bananas, sugar and egg. Beat until smooth.

Sift together flour, soda, baking powder, and salt.

Add these sifted dry ingredients and then the melted butter to the banana mixture. Mix at the lowest speed and only long enough to blend the ingredients.

Fill greased muffin tins ⅔ full.

Bake at 350 degrees for 15 minutes or until golden brown. For doneness test, see Graham Gems recipes above. Yield: 12 large muffins or 18 medium muffins.

Fall Tea

Tea   Coffee   Sherry

Open-faced Sandwiches:
Breast of Turkey with Cranberry or Mayonnaise
Chicken Liver Paté
Cucumber
Tomato and Green Pepper

Creamed Sweetbreads in Tart Shells

Hot Cream Scones with Concord Grape Jelly
and
Plum and Raisin Conserve
Pumpkin Nut Bread and Cranberry Loaf
Spicy Hermits and Date and Raisin Squares
Scripture Cake and Delicious Devil's Food Cake

In describing Canadian teas in the 1830's, Catherine Traill said, "Canada is the land of cakes. A tea table is generally furnished with several varieties of cakes and preserves." Nearly 150 years later, cakes and preserves still outnumber everything else in Canadian women's recipe collections. The cakes for this fall tea are two great Canadian favourites. Scripture cake and delicious devil's food are both nineteenth-century recipes; they include dried fruits and spices and have a slightly firm texture, so that they're at their best made in advance and left to mature a few days. Scripture cake was popular at pioneer quilting bees. The recipe was a guessing game in which the ingredients referred to Bible passages. The delicious devil's food remains an intriguing combination of chocolate, spices, and molasses.

1 loaf crusty homemade white
    bread (see basic recipes)
soft butter
cold roasted breast of turKey
    (see Thanksgiving dinner
    menu)
2 fine tomatoes
1 slim 6"-8" cucumber
½ green pepper
mayonnaise (see basic recipes)
cranberry sauce (see
    Thanksgiving dinner menu)
1 loaf stone-ground brown
    bread (see basic recipes)
butter
1 making chicken liver paté

Fall Tea Sandwiches

Cut the white bread into thin slices. Trim the crusts (save them for making into buttered crumbs or croutons). Butter evenly. Cut the turkey into thin slices. Remove the stem from the tomatoes and slice vertically. Rasp the skin of the cucumber and cut into very thin slices. Core the green pepper, remove the seeds, and cut into fine strips.

Cut each slice of buttered bread into thirds. On some lay the turkey, on some the slices of tomato, and on the rest the slices of cucumber. Lay strips of green pepper on the tomato sandwiches. Arrange on a large platter with small bowls of mayonnaise and cranberry sauce. Slice, toast, and butter the stone-ground brown bread. Cut each slice into thirds and arrange on a platter around a bowl of the chicken liver paté (see below).

For recipes for Concord grape jelly and plum and raisin conserve see the preserves section at the end of the book.

¼ cup butter
½ cup chopped onions
½ cup chopped, pared and
    cored apples
¼ cup butter
1 lb chicken livers, trimmed
    and cut in half
1 bay leaf
1 tsp salt
½ tsp freshly ground pepper
½ tsp dried crushed thyme or 1
    tsp chopped fresh thyme
½ tsp dried crushed marjoram
    or 1 tsp chopped fresh
    marjoram
2 tbsp heavy cream
¼ cup butter
2 tsp brandy
salt and pepper

Chicken Liver Paté

Melt the first ¼ cup butter in a frying pan. Add the onions and sauté over medium heat 3 minutes. Add the apples and continue cooking until the apples and onions are transparent. Pour into the container of a blender.

Melt the second ¼ cup butter, letting it foam up but not burn. Add the livers, bay leaf, salt, pepper, thyme, and marjoram. Sauté over moderate heat until the livers are browned but still slightly pink inside. Remove the bay leaf. Add the livers to the onions and apples in the blender. Blend, adding the cream, until the mixture is smooth.

For very smooth paste, press the blended liver mixture through a fine sieve. Cool. Soften the last ¼ cup butter. Gradually incorporate the liver mixture into the butter. Mix in the brandy and add salt and pepper to taste.

Pack into containers and press waxed paper or plastic wrap onto the top of the paste. Refrigerate at least 4 hours before serving.

Creamed Sweetbreads in Tart Shells

12-14 large tart shells or 24-28 small tart shells (see basic recipes)
1 lb veal sweetbreads
cold water
boiling water
1 tbsp vinegar or lemon juice
¼ cup butter
2 tbsp butter
2 cups sliced mushrooms
½ cup finely chopped onions
2 tbsp flour
½ cup white wine
1 tsp salt
½ tsp freshly ground pepper
1 cup medium cream
1 tbsp finely chopped parsley

Soak the sweetbreads in cold water to cover, 4 hours. Drain.

Simmer till firm in boiling water to cover and vinegar, about 7 minutes. Drain. Cool in cold running water. Slice into ½" cubes, removing any sinews. Melt the ¼ cup butter, add the sweetbreads, and sauté 12 minutes. Remove and reserve. Melt the 2 tbsp butter in the same pan. Add the mushrooms and onions. Cook over medium heat 4 minutes, shaking the saucepan frequently. Add the flour, stirring to coat the vegetables. Cook 2-3 minutes. Pour in the wine. Cook till the mixture thickens evenly, about 3-4 minutes, then add the salt, pepper, and cream and cook about 4 minutes more. Add the sweetbreads. Taste, add more salt if desired. Heat through and spoon into hot tart shells. Sprinkle with parsley.

Hot Cream Scones

2 ¼ cups sifted all-purpose flour
1 tbsp baking powder
2 tbsp white sugar
½ tsp salt
½ cup shortening or butter
2 eggs, lightly beaten
½ cup light cream
2 tbsp milk
1 tbsp white sugar

Sift together the flour, baking powder, 2 tbsp sugar, and salt. Cut in the shortening or butter with a pastry blender until the mixture is crumbly.

Combine the eggs and light cream.

Add the liquid ingredients to the dry, stirring lightly with a fork to combine. Turn out onto a floured board and knead lightly. Roll out ¾" thick.

Cut into diamonds or circles. Place scones on a lightly floured baking sheet. Brush the tops with milk and sprinkle with the 1 tbsp sugar.

Bake at 450 degrees 12-15 minutes until golden brown. Yield: 18 scones.
Serve while still hot.

2 cups sifted all-purpose flour
2 tsp baking powder
½ tsp soda
1 tsp salt
1 tsp cinnamon
½ tsp freshly grated nutmeg
1 cup cooked pumpkin purée
    (see basic recipes)
1 cup white sugar
½ cup milk
2 eggs, lightly beaten
¼ cup very soft butter
1 cup chopped pecans or
    walnuts

Pumpkin Nut Bread

Sift together flour, baking powder, soda, salt, cinnamon, and nutmeg.

Combine pumpkin, sugar, milk, and eggs in a large bowl. Add softened butter and then the dry ingredients. Mix until blended. Stir in nuts.

Pour into a well-greased loaf pan 9" x 4".

Bake one hour at 350 degrees or until a skewer inserted in the centre comes out clean.

Cool in the pan 10 minutes. Remove from the pan and cool on a rack. Wrap and store 1 day before slicing.

2 cups sifted all-purpose flour
1 ½ tsp baking powder
½ tsp soda
½ tsp salt
1 cup white sugar
grated rind of 1 orange
juice from 1 orange and enough
    water to make ¾ cup
1 egg, well beaten
2 tbsp butter, melted
1 cup quartered cranberries

Cranberry Loaf

Sift together the flour, baking powder, soda, salt, and sugar.

Combine the orange rind, juice, egg, melted butter, and cranberries. Stir into the dry ingredients. Mix until ingredients are well blended. Pour into a greased 9" x 4" loaf pan. Bake at 350 degrees 50 minutes or until a skewer inserted in the middle comes out clean.

Cool in pan 10 minutes. Remove from pan and cool on a rack. Wrap and store 1 day before slicing.

LEMON PEEL

Spicy Hermits

1 cup butter
1 cup firmly packed brown
    sugar
1 egg
1 tsp vanilla
1 ½ cups sifted all-purpose
    flour
½ tsp soda
¼ tsp salt
½ tsp ground allspice
¼ tsp ground cinnamon
¼ tsp ground cloves
3 cups dried fruits and nuts
    made up of 1 ½ cups
    chopped dates, 1 cup raisins,
    and ½ cup chopped walnuts

Cream butter till light and fluffy. Beat in the sugar and egg. Add vanilla.

Sift together the flour, soda, salt, and spices. Add to the creamed mixture.

Stir in the dried fruits and nuts.

Drop from a teaspoon onto greased baking sheets.

Bake at 350 degrees for 12 minutes. Yield: 6 dozen.

Date and Raisin Squares

Filling:
1 ½ cups chopped dates
1 ½ cups seeded raisins
⅓ cup white sugar
1 tsp grated lemon rind
2 tbsp lemon juice
⅛ tsp freshly grated nutmeg
1 ½ cups boiling water

Crumbs:
¾ cup butter
¾ cup firmly packed brown
    sugar
½ tsp vanilla
1 cup sifted all-purpose flour
½ tsp soda
½ tsp salt
2 ½ cups rolled oats

Combine all ingredients for the filling in a heavy-bottomed saucepan and simmer until the mixture is thick and the moisture absorbed. Cool.

Cream the butter till light and fluffy. Beat in the sugar. Add the vanilla.

Sift together the flour, soda, and salt; combine with the oats. Mix the dry ingredients into the beaten mixture to form big crumbs.

Put half the crumbs into the bottom of a well-greased 9" x 9" cake tin. Spread with the cooled date filling. Sprinkle on the rest of the crumbs.

Bake at 350 degrees for 40-45 minutes. Cool. Cut into squares.

½ cup butter
1 cup firmly packed brown
  sugar
3 eggs
2 tbsp honey
1¼ cups sifted cake flour
1 cup whole wheat flour
2 tsp baking powder
⅛ tsp salt
⅛ tsp each of ground cloves,
  ground allspice, and ground
  mace
½ tsp ground cinnamon
¼ tsp freshly grated nutmeg
1 cup seeded raisins
1 cup chopped figs
½ cup slivered almonds
6 tbsp milk

Sugar glaze:
½ cup icing sugar
2 tsp hot milk
¼ tsp vanilla

Scripture Cake

Prepare in advance a large loaf tin, 10" x 5", or a 9" tube pan. Grease very thoroughly. Then line the bottom of the pan with waxed paper, cut to fit. Grease the paper.

Preheat the oven to 325 degrees.

Cream the butter till light and fluffy. Gradually beat in the sugar. Add the eggs one at a time, beating well after each addition. Stir in the honey.

Stir together the cake and whole wheat flours, baking powder, salt, and spices. Use ⅓ cup to dredge the raisins, figs, and almonds. Take care to separate the pieces of dried fruit.

To the creamed mixture, add the dry ingredients in 3 parts alternating with the milk in 2 parts, beginning and ending with the dry ingredients. Stir in the dredged fruit and nuts.

Fill the pan with batter no more than ⅔ full. Drop the pan 2 to 3 inches onto the table. This spreads the batter into all the corners and eliminates air holes. Push the batter towards the edge of the pan, making a depression in the middle. This compensates for the naturally higher rise in the middle of the pan.

Bake at 325 degrees for 45 to 60 minutes, or until the cake tests for doneness. To test, insert a skewer into the centre of the cake. If it comes out clean, the cake is cooked. Or, touch the centre lightly; if the cake springs back, it is ready. The third test is to see if the cake has come away from the sides of the pan. Any cake which passes one of these tests will not fall once removed from the oven.

Cool 10 minutes in the pan. Then loosen sides with a knife and invert on a rack or racks, and cool thoroughly.

Combine icing sugar, hot milk, and vanilla. Drizzle on the cake quickly.

½ cup butter
½ cup firmly packed brown
   sugar
½ cup white sugar
2 eggs, separated
¼ cup molasses
2 cups sifted cake flour
½ tsp cream of tartar
¼ tsp soda
½ tsp ground cinnamon
½ tsp ground cloves
½ tsp ground allspice
½ tsp freshly grated nutmeg
¼ cup cocoa
¼ cup boiling water
½ cup milk
1 cup seeded raisins
½ cup mixed peel

Delicious Devil's Food

Prepare a deep 9″ x 9″ pan in advance, following the instructions in the previous recipe for scripture cake.

Preheat the oven to 350 degrees

Cream the butter until light and fluffy. Gradually beat in the sugar. Beat in the egg yolks one at a time. Reserve the whites. Add the molasses.

Sift together the flour, cream of tartar, soda, and spices. Dissolve cocoa in water and add milk.

Dredge the raisins and peel in ¼ cup of the sifted dry ingredients.

To the creamed mixture, add the dry ingredients in 3 parts alternately with the liquid in 2 parts, beginning and ending with the dry ingredients.

Beat the egg whites till stiff but not dry. Fold into the batter along with the dredged fruit. Spoon the batter into the pan, but ensure that the pan is no more than ⅔ full. Drop the pan 2 to 3 inches onto the table, and push the batter towards the edge of the pan as described in the scripture cake recipe.

Bake at 350 degrees for 50-60 minutes, or until the cake tests for doneness. Use the tests described in the scripture cake recipe. Cool 10 minutes in the pan. Then loosen sides with a knife and invert on a rack or racks, and cool thoroughly.

Ice with bittersweet chocolate icing (see below), or simply sprinkle the cake with icing sugar.

1 cup unsifted icing sugar
1 egg
2 tbsp soft butter
½ tsp vanilla
2 tbsp light cream
2 squares unsweetened
   chocolate, melted (2 oz)

Bittersweet Chocolate Icing for Delicious Devil's Food

Combine all ingredients in order given in a bowl. Place the bowl in a pan of ice cubes and water. Beat until thick and stiff with an electric beater.

Yield: enough to frost the top and sides of an 8″ or 9″ layer cake.

Baked Peameal Bacon Supper

Baked Peameal Bacon
Mustard Beans

Choice of:
Scalloped Tomatoes with Herbs
Baked Stuffed Tomatoes with Marjoram
Corn Oysters

Marinated Cauliflower Salad

Rosy Cranberry Apple Sauce
Oatmeal Date Cookies

Suggested beverage:
dry red wine or cold beer

This fall supper is built around a unique Canadian meat, peameal bacon, which is pickled but unsmoked loin of pork rolled in cornmeal. Usually it is sliced and fried for breakfast, but it is excellent baked whole. The cornmeal makes a crisp exterior and the meat, although quite lean, is particularly juicy because of the pickling process. For baking, it is important to select a piece from the centre cut, with a wide band of lean visible on both ends.

Tomatoes and/or corn are natural fall accompaniments. Scalloped tomatoes with herbs, butter, and crumbs is a real delicacy. Corn fritters are particularly light in Canada, where they are made with stiffly beaten egg white. Because of their irregular shape and size, many old cookbooks called them corn oysters.

The dessert may look standard, but the addition of cranberries makes ordinary apple sauce special and the oatmeal cookies studded with dates are—quite simply—marvelous.

1 centre-cut piece of peameal bacon (the leanest loin piece), 1 ½-2 lbs	# Baked Peameal Bacon

Place in open roasting pan, fat side up. Bake at 350 degrees for 1-1 ¼ hours. Serve hot in generous slices with mustard beans (see preserves recipes).

¼ cup butter
1 ½ cups sliced onions (3-4 medium)
1 ½ tsp white sugar
½ tsp salt
¼ tsp freshly ground pepper
½ tsp crushed dried thyme or 1 tsp chopped fresh thyme
2 cups coarse soft bread crumbs
2 tbsp finely chopped parsley
1 tsp finely chopped chives
6 large ripe tomatoes
2 tbsp butter

Scalloped Tomatoes with Herbs

Melt the ¼ cup butter over medium heat. Add onions, sugar, salt, pepper, and thyme. Stir. Cook 4-5 minutes or until the onions are transparent but not brown. Remove from the heat.

Combine the bread crumbs, parsley and chives. Toss lightly.

Stir half the bread crumb mixture into the onions. Cut tomatoes into ½" slices. Arrange alternate layers of tomatoes and the onion mixture in a buttered, ovenproof dish, ending with tomatoes on top. Sprinkle on remaining plain bread crumbs and dot with 2 tbsp butter.

Bake at 350 degrees 35-45 minutes or until the tomatoes are tender and the top is crisp. Serve immediately.

6 medium tomatoes
salt
2 cups plus 2 tbsp stale but not dry bread crumbs or cubes
1 ½ tbsp parsley, finely chopped
1 ½ tbsp chives or green onion tops, finely chopped

a few gratings of nutmeg
¾ tsp salt
½ tsp freshly ground pepper
1 tsp chopped fresh marjoram or ½ tsp dried crushed marjoram
6 tbsp butter, melted

Baked Stuffed Tomatoes with Marjoram

Wash tomatoes. With a sharp knife cut a 1 ½" to 2" circle out of the stem end. Scoop out the pulp. (Use pulp for another purpose such as soup.) Salt the insides lightly. Turn upside down on a plate to drain for one hour.

Combine the rest of the ingredients. Toss well to distribute the butter and sweet herbs.

Fill the tomatoes with stuffing, mounding it on the top. Place side by side in a buttered baking dish.

Bake 25-30 minutes at 350 degrees. If necessary, grill for 2-3 minutes at the end in order to brown the crumbs. Do not overcook or the tomatoes will fall apart. Serve immediately.

2 eggs
2 cups cooked corn niblets or
   fresh cut from the cob
2 tbsp flour
½ tsp salt
¼ tsp freshly ground pepper
a few gratings of nutmeg

Corn Oysters

Separate eggs. Beat whites until stiff, but not dry. Combine the corn, yolks, flour, and seasonings. Fold in the whites. Drop by teaspoonfuls onto a hot buttered frying pan. Brown and turn once.

1 medium cauliflower, about
   1 ½ lbs
5-6 cups cold water
1 ½ tsp lemon juice
boiling water
1 tsp salt
½ cup olive oil
2 tbsp lemon juice
2 tsp cider vinegar
½ tsp salt
½ tsp freshly ground pepper
1 medium clove of garlic, finely
   chopped
3 tbsp finely chopped parsley
3 tbsp finely chopped green
   onions or chives

Marinated Cauliflower Salad

Trim cauliflower. Break into medium flowerets. Soak 1 hour in cold water and lemon juice. Drain.

Place in a saucepan and pour in boiling water, about ¾ way up the flowerets. Add 1 tsp salt. Simmer uncovered 10-12 minutes or until just tender. Drain. Dry briefly on paper towel. Place in bowl.

Combine the rest of the ingredients and pour over cauliflower while still warm. Toss lightly, chill, toss lightly again before serving.

6 large apples (Northern Spies
   are good)
½ cup uncooked cranberries
⅓ cup cider or water
6 tbsp honey or white sugar

Rosy Cranberry Apple Sauce

Wash and cut apples into quarters. Do not core or peel. Place in a saucepan that has a tight-fitting lid. Add the cranberries and cider. Simmer covered 15-20 minutes, stirring and mashing periodically until the apples are soft and the cranberries have popped. Put through a food mill or push through a sieve. Add honey. Taste, add more sweetening if desired. Chill.

¾ cup butter
1 cup firmly packed brown
   sugar
1 cup white sugar
2 eggs
½ tsp vanilla
1 ¾ cups sifted all-purpose
   flour
1 tsp soda
½ tsp salt
2 cups rolled oats
1 cup finely chopped dates

Oatmeal Date Cookies

Cream butter till light and fluffy. Gradually add the brown and white sugar, beating well. Add the eggs one at a time, beating after each addition. Add the vanilla.

Sift together the flour, soda, and salt. Add to the creamed mixture. Work in the rolled oats and dates. Shape into a roll 2 ½" in diameter. Chill overnight. Cut into ½" slices and place on a greased baking sheet.

Bake at 375 degrees for 10 minutes or until golden brown on the bottom. Remove from the pan and cool on a rack.

Hallowe'en Candies and Treats

Prize Maple Cream Fudge

Butterscotch

Old-fashioned Molasses Pull Taffy

Peanut Brittle

Molasses Popcorn Balls

Candy Apples

Potato Doughnuts with Cinnamon Sugar

Mulled Apple Cider

Hallowe'en is the perfect occasion for homemade candy. The recipes included here are all long-standing favourites. Candies were once quite complicated to make, what with all the guess-work involved in determining the various stages of the cooking progress, but the candy thermometer changed all that. Fudge is probably the most common homemade candy. At one time toffee was a close second. The original maple cream fudge was indeed made from maple syrup or maple sugar, and brown sugar is certainly an inferior substitute. Another change in the times involves molasses; traditionally it was *the* syrup in popcorn balls, caramels, toffee, and butterscotch, but milder-tasting corn syrup now often replaces it.

The candy treat most nostalgically associated with Hallowe'en and fall fairs is candy apples. Just-harvested McIntosh apples are best for candy apples. Their juicy tart flesh is a perfect foil for the crunchy sweet coating, and their bright red colour shows through the candy. The rest of the candy you can make all year, but make these only when apples are at their best.

For reliable results in candy making, a candy thermometer is essential. In all the recipes which follow, temperature instructions are included.

3 cups firmly packed brown
    sugar
1 tbsp flour
⅛ tsp salt
3 tbsp butter
⅔ cup light cream
1 tsp vanilla
½ cup chopped nuts or ginger
    in syrup

Prize Maple Cream Fudge

Mix the sugar, flour, and salt in a saucepan. Add the butter and light cream. Stir to dissolve the sugar. Bring to the boil.

Continue cooking without stirring until the mixture reaches the softball stage, 238 degrees. Remove from the heat, and without stirring or agitating the saucepan, cool until barely luke-warm (110 degrees). Add vanilla.

Beat with a wooden spoon or electric mixer until creamy, thick, and no longer glossy.

Pour into a well-greased 8″ x 8″ cake tin.

While still warm, cut into squares. Press a nut or piece of drained ginger onto each square. Yield: about 2 lbs.

2 cups firmly packed brown
    sugar
¼ cup molasses or corn syrup
2 tbsp water
2 tbsp vinegar
½ cup butter

Butterscotch

Combine all the ingredients except butter in a saucepan. Heat slowly until the sugar is dissolved. Add butter. Boil over moderate heat without stirring to the hard-crack stage, 300 degrees. Pour onto a well-buttered marble slab or tray. Score into pieces while still warm. When cold, break into pieces along the scored lines. Wrap pieces in waxed paper and store in a container with a tight-fitting lid.

Yield: about 1 lb.

2 cups firmly packed brown
    sugar
½ cup water
⅛ tsp cream of tartar
¼ cup molasses
2 tbsp butter
1 tsp vinegar
1 tsp vanilla

Old-fashioned Molasses Pull Taffy

Combine the sugar, water, and cream of tartar in a heavy-bottomed saucepan. Stir together over low heat until the sugar dissolves. Cover, boil 3 minutes, uncover. Boil slowly 9 minutes without stirring. Add the molasses, butter, and vinegar. Boil over medium heat to the hard-crack stage, 300 degrees. Add the vanilla. Pour immediately onto a large, well-greased tray or marble slab. As the edge of the candy firms and cools, turn it into the centre with a spatula. When cool enough to handle, butter your hands, roll the candy into a ball, and pull the taffy until it is beautifully straw-coloured. Pull and twist into ropes ¾″ in diameter. Cut into ½″ pieces with greased kitchen shears. Cool and wrap pieces individually in waxed paper.

Yield: about 1 lb.

Peanut Brittle

2 cups white sugar
½ cup water
1 cup corn syrup
2 cups raw shelled peanuts
½ tsp salt
2 tbsp butter
½ tsp soda

Combine the sugar, water, and corn syrup in a heavy-bottomed saucepan. Bring to the boil. Cover and cook 3 minutes. Uncover, add the peanuts, and cook without stirring to the soft-crack stage, 280 degrees. Add the salt and the butter, and continue cooking and stirring constantly to the hard-crack stage, 300 degrees. Add the soda. Spread quickly onto a large, very well-greased tray or marble slab. Using 2 wooden spoons, spread the hot candy as thin as it will go without separating. Cool and break into pieces. Store in a tight-fitting container.

Yield: about 2 ½ lbs.

Molasses Popcorn Balls

2 cups popcorn, unpopped
¼ cup oil (optional)
2 tbsp butter
1 cup white sugar
1 cup molasses
½ tsp salt

Pop the corn, ½ cup at a time, in an open wire popper or in a covered pan, using 1 tbsp of oil with each popping. Pour the popped corn into a very large buttered bowl.

Melt the butter in a large saucepan. Add the sugar, molasses, and salt. Bring to the boil. Cover and cook 3 minutes. Remove lid and continue cooking over moderate heat to the hard-ball stage (260 degrees).

Immediately pour over the corn, stirring the corn all the time with a large spoon to mix in the syrup.

Butter your hands generously and shape the popcorn into about 36 balls.

Wrap in waxed paper.

Candy Apples

10-12 medium apples, bright red (McIntosh are best)
10-12 wooden skewers
3 cups white sugar
1 cup water
¼ tsp cream of tartar
2 whole cloves
10 drops red food colouring

Wash and polish apples. Insert skewers into stem end. Prepare squares of waxed paper or tinfoil each big enough to hold an apple, blossom end down. Boil 1″ of water in a large flat pan.

Place the rest of the ingredients into a heavy-bottomed sauce-pan that will fit into the flat pan. Stir over low direct heat to dissolve the sugar, then, without stirring, continue cooking over moderate heat to the medium-crack stage (290 degrees). Remove from heat. Place in the pan of hot water. Dip apples quickly into the syrup and set, skewer end up, on the waxed paper squares. Let cool.

1 cup thoroughly mashed
  potatoes
1 cup white sugar
2 eggs, lightly beaten
1 tbsp melted butter
2 ½ cups sifted all-purpose
  flour
2 ½ tsp baking powder
½ tsp salt
½ tsp freshly grated nutmeg
½ cup milk minus 1 tbsp
2 tbsp flour for rolling out
fine granulated sugar,
  cinnamon, nutmeg

Potato Doughnuts with Cinnamon Sugar

Combine the mashed potatoes, 1 cup sugar, eggs, and melted butter.

Sift together the 2 ½ cups flour, baking powder, salt, and nutmeg.

Add these dry ingredients alternately with the milk to the potato mixture.

Refrigerate at least ½ hour. Remove ½ the dough from the refrigerator. Using 1 tbsp of flour, roll out to ½" thick. Cut out with a floured 3" doughnut cutter.

Fry in 2" of fat at 360 degrees, making sure the fat does not get too hot. The doughnuts need at least 3 minutes cooking in order to be done through. Turn once during cooking. Repeat with second half.

Drain on paper towel. Sprinkle lavishly with the sugar and spices.

Yield: about 2 ½ dozen.

1 tsp whole cloves
1 tsp whole allspice
1 cinnamon stick, cracked
8 cups fresh cider
½ cup firmly packed brown
  sugar

Mulled Apple Cider

Tie the spices in a piece of rinsed cheesecloth. Simmer together with the cider and brown sugar for 20 minutes. Discard the spice bag. Pour into mugs.

Winter

Tiger Dunlop had a wry view of the seasons in Canada. "For two months of the spring and two months of the autumn, you are up to your middle in mud; for four months of summer, you are broiled by the heat, choked by the dust and devoured by the mosquitoes; and for the remaining four months, if you get your nose above the snow, it is to have it bit off by the frost." He wrote this in 1842 in a book called *Upper Canada*, but his description still applies fairly accurately—except for the coast of British Columbia—to the climate of the whole country.

Canadians have had two reactions to the winter. Some have hated the cold, the snow, the ice, the lack of fresh fruits and vegetables, and the inconvenience. Others, like Catherine Traill, have seen it as a welcome change: "January parties, balls, picnics and sleigh rides are frequent in the towns and long settled parts of the country; so that though the cold is often intense this season is not without its pleasures."

In nineteenth-century rural Canada, winter meant relaxation from the pressures of plowing, growing, and harvesting. A good snowfall signified sleighing, and considering the lamentable state of the roads of that time, this was the easiest and fastest method of transportation. Visiting back and forth was therefore easier in winter, and there was also time for it.

Our major feasts and holidays take place in the winter. Christmas and New Year's, for many people, are the focal point of the whole year. Discussions start months in advance about when to bake the cake or the shortbread, how to make the mincemeat, or whether to have turkey or goose. More than at any other time, people are conscious of tradition and quality in what they eat. They will cheerfully indulge in oysters, or the best fruit for the cake, or the finest fowl, or their favourite wine because— after all—"it's only once a year". In fact, the look and spirit of the winter holiday hasn't changed much since Susanna Moodie described it in *Life in the Clearings:*

> It was the Christmas week, and the market was adorned with evergreens, and dressed with all possible care. The stalls groaned beneath the weight of good cheer—fish, flesh, and fowl, all contributing their share to tempt the appetite and abstract money from the purse. It was a sight to warm the heart of the most fastidious epicure and give him the nightmare for the next seven nights, only dreaming of that stupendous quantity of food to be masticated by the jaws of man.

After New Year's, there are still three months left of Canadian winter. To think positively, however, these are wonderful months for eating: long-simmered soups, robust oven dinners, roasts, and spicy desserts.

The very limitations of winter can act as a creative charge to Canadian cooks, as the recipes in this section will hopefully show.

Christmas Dinner

Fresh Oysters on the Half Shell
Stone-ground Brown Bread and Sweet Butter

Christmas Goose with Transparent Spiced Apples
Butter Crumb Creamed Onions
Honey Glazed Carrots
Whipped Herbed Potatoes

Christmas Plum Pudding with Hard Sauce or Brandy or Rum
Sauce
Christmas Carrot Pudding

Suggested beverage with the oysters:
chilled white wine or ale

Suggested beverage with the goose:
chilled white, chilled rosé, or full-bodied red wine

To begin this special dinner, serve oysters on their own shells in their own liquor. This is the real way to appreciate their delicate flavour. All they need is a few drops of lemon juice, plus some thin slices of stone-ground brown bread and sweet butter.

For the main course, I bow to the custom of having goose for Christmas. It is more expensive than turkey, and it will not by itself serve more than six to ten people; but as a once-a-year treat, it is unbeatable.

Carrots and onions are the most satisfactorily stored vegetables, though that is not reason enough to choose them for this menu. The glazing of one and the creaming of the other, however, turn them into rare Christmas offerings. A preliminary cooking in chicken stock is important for their flavour.

Since this is undoubtedly the most traditional of all meals, it is fitting to end it with an old-fashioned steamed fruit pudding. If you choose the plum pudding, which is as rich as possible, flame it and serve it with brandy or hard sauce. If you decide on the authentic Canadian carrot pudding, serve it with a jug of caramel sauce and a jug of heavy cream.

6 oysters per person, opened just before serving
chipped ice
2 lemons, cut in wedges, seeded
6-8 thin slices stone-ground brown bread (see basic recipes)
sweet butter
peppermill

Fresh Oysters on the Half Shell

To open the oysters, scrub the shells and hold over a bowl in a folded cloth, the deep shell down. Insert the oyster knife into the hinge, pry open, cut the hinge muscle, and work the knife around to open the shells. Any juice that has escaped should be poured over the oysters. Lay the oysters in their deep shell on the cracked ice. Arrange the lemon wedges around the oysters.

Trim the crusts from the bread. Butter each slice and cut into three fingers. Pass the peppermill with the oysters.

1 goose, 7-11 lbs
½ tsp salt
stuffing (see below)
salt

Pan Gravy:
2 tbsp drippings from roasting pan
2 tbsp flour
1 ½ cups cider, water, or chicken stock (see basic recipes)
salt
pepper
2 tbsp port

Christmas Goose with Transparent Spiced Apples

Remove any pin feathers with tweezers. Cut out the oil sac at the base of the tail. Wipe inside of goose with a damp cloth and sprinkle lightly with ½ tsp salt.

Make stuffing. Loosely stuff the body and neck cavities of the goose. Fasten the edges together with skewers or sew with thread and needle. Tie the legs together with string. Bind the wings close to the body. Prick the goose all over with a fork. Place breast up on a rack in a shallow, uncovered roasting pan.

Roast at 325 degrees uncovered without basting, 30 minutes per pound for a 7 to 8-lb goose and 25 minutes per pound for a 9 to 11-lb goose. Remove excess fat as it accumulates. Prick the goose several times lightly during the cooking to release excess fat.

When the goose is done, salt lightly and place on a large preheated platter in a warm place and leave for 10 minutes while you make the gravy. This resting period sets the meat and makes it easier to carve.

Remove all but 2 tbsp of the drippings from the roasting pan. Blend in flour, using a wooden spoon. When the mixture is a smooth paste, place over medium heat. Slowly add the liquid, stirring constantly to prevent lumps.

At this stage, a whisk is excellent.

Taste. Add salt and pepper if necessary. Add the port. Strain into a warmed gravy boat and serve immediately.

Serve the goose garnished with parsley and surrounded by transparent spiced apples (see preserves recipes at end of book).

⅓ cup butter
¾ cup finely chopped onions
3 cups cored and chopped apples
½ cup raisins (seedless are best)
2 tbsp finely chopped parsley
1 tsp salt
¼ tsp freshly ground pepper
⅛ tsp ground cinnamon
½ tsp crushed dried sage
¼ tsp crushed dried thyme
¼ tsp crushed dried basil
5 cups soft stale bread crumbs
3 tbsp brown sugar

Stuffing for the Goose

Melt the butter in a large frying pan. Sauté the onions over low heat about 5 minutes or until barely transparent.

Add the apples, raisins, and seasonings. Continue cooking over moderate heat 5 minutes. Pour this savoury mixture over the bread crumbs and brown sugar. Toss well. Divide the stuffing roughly, ⅓ for the neck cavity and ⅔ for the body. Pack in lightly and skewer shut.

This is plenty of stuffing for a 7 to 8-lb goose. For a larger goose, increase the bread to 7 cups, the butter to ½ cup, the onions to 1 cup, and the salt to 1 ½ tsp.

12 medium onions (1 ¾ lbs)
1 cup lightly salted chicken stock (see basic recipes)

Cream Sauce:
2 tbsp butter
2 tbsp flour
¾ cup onion cooking liquid (make up quantity with water if necessary)
⅛ tsp freshly grated nutmeg
½ cup light cream
salt

Crumbs:
2 tbsp butter
4 tbsp crisp bread crumbs

Butter Crumb Creamed Onions

Peel onions and cut a shallow X in the bottom. Place the onions in one layer in a saucepan. Add the stock, cover, bring to the boil, reduce heat, and cook 30-40 minutes or until tender. Drain well, reserving the cooking liquid. Place onions in a greased, shallow, ovenproof dish.

Melt the butter for the cream sauce, stir in the flour, and cook over low heat 3-4 minutes. Gradually add the hot onion cooking liquid, stirring until the sauce thickens smoothly. Add the nutmeg and cream. Taste. Add more salt if necessary. Spoon sauce evenly over the onions.

Melt the last 2 tbsp butter in a frying pan. Add the bread crumbs. Stir over medium heat 3-4 minutes to lightly brown the crumbs. Sprinkle over the creamed onions.

Set in a 375-degree oven for 10 minutes or until the sauce bubbles up around the onions and the top is lightly browned.

Honey Glazed Carrots

1 ½ lbs small carrots (2 bunches)
cold water
¼ cup butter
⅓ cup chicken stock (see basic recipes)
4 tsp honey
¼ tsp salt

Scrape carrots. Leave whole. Place in a saucepan and cover with cold water. Cover the saucepan. Bring to the boil and drain immediately.

Return carrots to the saucepan. Add the butter, stock, honey, and salt.

Simmer covered 10 minutes. Uncover. Simmer about 5 minutes more or until the liquid is absorbed and the carrots slightly browned and tender. Turn the carrots in the last 5 minutes to brown evenly. Place in a preheated serving dish.

Whipped Herbed Potatoes

6 medium potatoes, 2-2 ½ lbs
boiling water
1 tsp salt
1 cup light cream
½ cup milk
2 tbsp butter
2 tbsp finely chopped green onions or chives
2 tbsp finely chopped parsley
¼ tsp freshly ground pepper
salt

Peel potatoes and divide in quarters. Cover with boiling water. Add salt, boil 20 minutes or until tender. Drain. Return to saucepan and shake dry over heat. Mash very well.

Scald cream and milk. Beat into the potatoes with the butter. It should be a light and smooth purée. Add onions, parsley, and pepper. Taste. Add more salt if necessary.

Place in a greased, shallow, ovenproof dish. Smooth the top and draw a lattice pattern on it with a knife. Place under the grill until lightly browned, 3-4 minutes. Serve.

½ cup butter
1 cup plus 2 tbsp firmly packed
  brown sugar
½ cup grated suet
3 eggs
1 cup sifted all-purpose flour
1 tsp soda
1 tsp salt
½ tsp freshly grated nutmeg
½ tsp ground cloves
1 tsp ground cinnamon
¼ tsp ground mace
1 ½ cups seeded raisins
1 cup seedless raisins
⅓ cup chopped candied
  orange peel
⅓ cup chopped candied lemon
  peel
⅓ cup chopped candied citron
  peel
½ cup halved glacé cherries
½ cup almond slivers
1 cup fine, soft, but stale bread
  crumbs
½ cup rum or brandy
¼ cup rum or brandy, for
  flaming

Christmas Plum Pudding

Cream the butter and sugar until light and fluffy. Mix in the suet. Beat in the eggs one at a time.

Sift together the flour, soda, salt, and spices. Combine the fruits and nuts. Dredge with ½ cup of the sifted dry ingredients. Add the bread crumbs to the remaining dry ingredients.

Add the dry ingredients in 3 parts alternately with the ½ cup of rum in 2 parts to the creamed mixture. Begin and end with the dry ingredients. Mix in the fruit and nuts. Spoon into a greased, 2-quart mould. Cover with a piece of aluminum foil that has a 1" pleat so the pudding can rise. Tie firmly around the rim with string.

Place on a rack in a steamer. Fill the steamer ⅔ of the way up the mould with boiling water. Cover, bring to the boil, reduce heat, and boil moderately 2 ½ hours. Add more boiling water periodically to maintain the level. Remove and cool. Leave the original aluminum foil on the top, wrap in plastic wrap and keep refrigerated until it is to be eaten. A pudding will keep well in the refrigerator 3-4 weeks, and 3 months in the freezer. Remove the plastic wrap before resteaming and replace the aluminum foil on the top if it has any holes or rips.

To serve, steam again 1 hour. Remove from the steamer, let stand 5 minutes, unmould. Warm the ¼ cup rum or brandy, ignite, and pour over the pudding. Serve with hard sauce or rum or brandy sauce, depending on the liquor used in the pudding and flaming. For instance, if you use rum in the pudding, flame the pudding in rum and use it to flavour the sauce. Ditto with the brandy.

⅓ cup soft butter
1 cup firmly packed brown
  sugar
2 tsp brandy or dark rum
a grate of nutmeg

Hard Sauce

Cream the butter till fluffy. Work in the sugar and beat till light. Beat in the brandy, gradually, and add the nutmeg. Pack into a small crock or dish. Chill and serve with plum pudding.

¼ cup butter
1 cup firmly packed brown
  sugar
2 egg yolks
2 tbsp brandy or rum
1 cup light cream
2 egg whites

Brandy or Rum Sauce

Combine butter and brown sugar in the top of a double boiler. Add egg yolks. Beat well. Slowly add brandy or rum and light cream, stirring to prevent lumps.

Cook over gently boiling water until thick and smooth.

Beat egg whites until they are stiff but not dry. Slowly pour the hot mixture over the egg whites, stirring gently. Pour into a jug. Serve immediately with the plum pudding or the carrot pudding.

1 cup grated peeled carrots
1 cup grated peeled potatoes
1 cup finely shredded suet
1 cup raisins, preferably seeded
1 cup currants
½ cup mixed chopped candied
  peel
½ cup glacé cherries, cut in half
1 ¼ cups firmly packed brown
  sugar
1 ½ cups sifted all-purpose
  flour
1 tsp soda
1 tsp salt
1 tsp ground cinnamon
½ tsp freshly grated nutmeg
¼ tsp ground allspice or cloves
¼ cup brandy or rum, for
  flaming
caramel sauce (see below)

Christmas Carrot Pudding

Combine carrots, potatoes, suet, raisins, currants, peel, cherries, and brown sugar. Sift together the flour, soda, salt, and spices. Work into the other ingredients. Pack into a well-greased pudding bowl, mould, or can. Grease one side of waxed paper cut to fit over the top of the pudding. Place the greased side over the pudding. Cover container with aluminum foil with a 1" pleat so the pudding can rise. Tie firmly with string around the rim.

Place on a rack in a large saucepan. Pour boiling water around the pudding ⅔ of the way up the pudding container. Cover and steam 3 hours. Periodically add more boiling water up to the original level.

Remove pudding container from the large saucepan. Cool. Wrap well and store in a cool dry place as for plum pudding. Steam 1 hour on the day of serving in a covered container.

Unmould onto a serving platter. Warm the brandy slightly. Ignite and pour over the pudding.

Serve with caramel sauce and heavy cream or brandy or rum sauce.

1 ½ cups brown sugar
2 cups boiling water
3 tbsp cornstarch
¼ tsp salt
2 tbsp cold water
3 tbsp butter
1 tsp vanilla
½ tsp freshly grated nutmeg
2 tbsp sweet sherry or port

Caramel Sauce for Steamed Puddings

Melt sugar in a heavy-bottomed saucepan over medium heat. Let brown slightly. Stir in the boiling water. Cook over medium heat until smooth and all the hard particles have dissolved.

Make a paste of the cornstarch, salt, and cold water. Gradually add to the sauce, stirring to prevent lumps and simmering until the taste of raw cornstarch disappears.

Remove from the heat. Stir in the butter, vanilla, nutmeg, sherry or port.

Yield: about 2 ½-3 cups sauce.

Christmas Treats

Rich Dark Fruit Cake with Butter Icing and Almond Icing

Glazed White Fruit Cake

Traditional Shortbread

Brandy Snaps

Swedish Tea Rings

Almond Crescents

Rich Pecan Squares

Very Hot Ginger Snaps

Almond Stuffed Dates

There are two distinct sorts of Christmas cakes, or fruit cakes: the dark, a rich cake with seeded raisins, nuts, and fruit that has hardly any batter; and the light, a much cakier creation with golden raisins, almonds, and light-coloured fruit. The dark should be made by mid-November in order to leave time for the flavours to blend and, what is more important, for the ritual sprinkling with rum or brandy. The light should be made three to four weeks before Christmas.

Since both these cakes are stored longer than most baked goods, the freshness of the ingredients is vital. This is especially true of the nuts. For best results, buy the nuts in their shells and shell them yourself. The same goes for the fruit. Peel and pineapple sold in big pieces may need to be chopped before being used, but the plus they provide in fresh flavour is worth the effort.

Store the cakes well wrapped in aluminum foil in containers with tight-fitting lids. A real fruit cellar where it is cool, dark, and dry is the ideal place. Every week or so, douse the dark cake with 2 tbsp of rum, brandy, or sherry. One way to assure even penetration is to make holes in the cake with a thin knitting needle or skewer at 2" to 3" intervals. The liquor will run in easily.

As for icing, all the light cake needs is a corn syrup glaze brushed on at the end of the baking period or an icing sugar glaze drizzled over the cake before serving. The latter is especially pretty if the cake is made in a tube pan and set on an old-fashioned cake stand.

Classically, the dark cake has a layer of almond icing and then a hard royal icing meant to keep in the moisture. However, as the latter has little flavour and often breaks up unattractively when the cake is cut, a rich butter icing is better. If you ice your cake in the week before Christmas and keep it in a container with a tight-fitting lid, it won't need the hard frosting.

The best-known of the Christmas cookies is shortbread, and delicious variations in the same family include Swedish tea rings and almond crescents. The best contrast in flavour and texture to these is ginger snaps, which can be cut into circles or into gingerbread men. For the latter, make a hole in the head and pipe on features and clothes with an icing sugar glaze so that they can be hung on the Christmas tree. Brandy snaps are lacy rolls of crunchy caramel around whipped cream. They have an undeserved reputation for being hard to make, for although the first few may be hard to manage, practice quickly makes perfect.

1 lb candied pineapple rings
½ lb candied cherries
¼ lb candied citron peel
⅛ lb candied lemon peel
⅛ lb candied orange peel
1 lb golden seedless raisins
¾ lb seeded raisins
½ cup brandy or rum
¼ lb blanched almonds
¼ lb pecan halves
½ cup butter
1 cup white sugar
1 cup firmly packed brown
    sugar
5 eggs
1 tsp almond extract
2 cups sifted all-purpose flour
½ tsp soda
½ tsp ground mace
½ tsp ground cinnamon
1 tbsp milk

Rich Dark Fruit Cake with Butter Icing and Almond Icing

Chop the pineapple into ¼" slices, the cherries in half, and the peel into ¼" pieces. Combine chopped fruit and raisins. Pour over the brandy, stir well. Cover and leave overnight. Stir once or twice.

Chop almonds into slivers. Combine with the pecans.

The next day prepare the pans. This amount of batter will make 1 large 8" x 8" x 3 ½" cake or 2 smaller ones, 6" x 6" x 3 ¼" and 4" x 4" x 3". Line the pan or pans with two layers of heavy brown paper and one layer of waxed paper. Grease the waxed paper.

Cream the butter until light and fluffy. Gradually add the sugar, beating well. Beat in the eggs, one at a time. Add the almond extract.

Sift the flour, soda, and spices. Remove 2 tbsp. Use to dredge the nuts. Add half the sifted dry ingredients, then the milk, and then the rest of the sifted ingredients to the batter. Stir in the fruit and nuts. Mix with your hands if necessary.

Spoon into the pan or pans. Bake at 275 degrees for 3 ¼ hours for a large cake, 2-2 ½ hours for the medium, and 1-1 ½ hours for the small cake or until a skewer inserted in the middle comes out clean and the cake is firm to the touch. Place a shallow pan of water in the oven during the cooking period to keep the cake moist.

Cool 10 minutes. Remove from the pans. Cool thoroughly on a rack. Remove the brown paper and waxed paper, wrap with aluminum foil, and store in a tight-fitting container in a cool place. Lace the cake periodically with a few tablespoons of brandy, rum, or sherry.

During the week before Christmas, cover with a ¼" layer of almond paste and butter icing. Store in a tight-fitting container.

Yield: 6 lbs of fruit cake.

¼ cup butter
2 cups sifted icing sugar
3 tbsp heavy cream
½ tsp almond extract

Butter Icing

Cream the butter. Add 2 tbsp of the sugar. Gradually add the cream and almond extract. Add the icing sugar to make a thick icing. More sugar may be added if necessary. Spread over the top and part way down the sides of the cake. Decorate with holly.

1 lb fresh blanched almonds
1 lb sifted icing sugar
3 egg whites, lightly beaten
1 tsp almond extract
1 tbsp rose water
1 egg white, lightly beaten

Almond Icing

Put the almonds through the finest blade of a food grinder. Work the next 4 ingredients into the almonds. Mix well, using your hands if necessary to make a smooth paste. Sprinkle board generously with icing sugar. Place almond icing on it. Roll out to the size of the fruit cake.

To ice the cake, brush the surface of the cake with the remaining beaten egg white. Place on the almond icing. Press down. Let stand 24 hours before frosting with butter icing.

2 cups almonds, blanched and slivered (½ lb)
3 cups golden seeded raisins or golden sultana raisins (1 lb)
1 cup desiccated cocoanut
1 ring of candied pineapple
½ cup chopped candied orange peel   ¼ lb)
1 cup candied red and green cherries (½ lb)
6 tbsp flour (for dredging fruits)
1 cup butter
1 cup white sugar
4 eggs, separated
1 tsp vanilla
1 tsp rose water or orange flower water
½ cup sherry
2 cups sifted all-purpose flour
1 ½ tsp baking powder
½ tsp salt
1 tsp freshly grated nutmeg

Glaze:
1 tbsp corn syrup
1 tsp water

Glazed White Fruit Cake

Mix together the nuts and fruit. Toss them with the 6 tbsp flour to coat evenly.

Cream butter and sugar together until light and fluffy. Add the egg yolks. Beat 5 minutes until the mixture is very fluffy. Add the vanilla, rose water and sherry. Beat again for about 1 minute.

Sift together the flour, baking powder, salt and nutmeg.

Beat the egg whites until they are stiff but not dry.

Stir the flour mixture into the creamed mixture alternately with the fruit and nuts.

Fold in the stiffly beaten egg whites.

Line one 7 ½″ x 7 ½″ fruit cake pan or two 9″ x 5″ loaf pans or a 9″ tube pan with four thicknesses of waxed paper. Butter the last layer.

Pour batter into pans and bake at 275 degrees 2 ½-3 hours or until a skewer inserted in the middle of the cake comes out clean.

Cool the cake thoroughly. Remove the waxed paper. Wrap in foil and store in a closely covered tin.

Glaze:
15 minutes before the end of the baking time, at 2 ¾ hours, remove cake from the oven. Combine the corn syrup and water and spread over the top. When the cake comes out, it will have a very nice glaze.

Alternately, do not glaze with corn syrup. Cool the cake and before serving, drizzle on an icing sugar glaze as on the scripture cake, page 125.

2 cups soft butter
½ cup firmly packed brown
  sugar
½ cup white sugar
3 cups sifted all-purpose flour
1 cup rice flour (or a fourth cup
  of sifted all-purpose flour)

Traditional Shortbread

Cream butter and sugars thoroughly. Add the all-purpose and the rice flour, mixing first with a spoon and later, as the mixture thickens, with your hands. The mixture should be smooth and satiny. Chill the dough a few minutes if it is soft; otherwise proceed.

Turn the dough out onto a lightly floured board and knead lightly for a few minutes.

Roll dough ½" thick. You have a whole range of possibilities for the shape of the shortbread. If you cut out 2" round cookies, you will get about 5 dozen. Or, you may like the traditional shape, which is a round of shortbread 8" in diameter. Flute the edges as you would a pie and mark into wedges with a knife and prick each wedge twice with a fork. When it is baked break into pieces along the marked wedges. Or you can simply square off the entire dough, cut it into squares or diamonds with a sharp knife, and prick each piece.

Bake at 275 degrees for about 35 minutes. The shortbread should be only lightly browned. Store in a container with a tight-fitting lid.

Brandy Snaps

½ cup butter
½ cup very firmly packed brown sugar
½ cup corn syrup
1 cup minus 1 tbsp flour
1 tsp ground ginger
1 tsp lemon juice
⅛ tsp vanilla
½ pint heavy cream

Put the butter, sugar, and syrup into a saucepan. Heat over medium heat until the butter has melted and the sugar dissolved. Let cool slightly. Sift together the flour and ginger. Add the dry ingredients, lemon juice, and vanilla to the butter mixture, stirring in well.

Drop by the teaspoon at least 4″ apart onto a well-greased baking sheet.

Bake at 325 degrees for 8 minutes. Remove from the oven, let set 2-3 minutes to firm up, remove from the pan with a turner or spatula, and roll up evenly one at a time around a small broom handle. If the brandy snaps get too hard to roll, set back in the oven a few seconds to soften. Cool on a rack. Store in an airtight container as soon as they are cold.

Yield: about 20 brandy snaps.

When serving, whip the heavy cream and fill the brandy snaps. The best way to fill them is with a piping bag and a star tip, but it is possible to fill them using a teaspoon and smoothing out the ends.

Swedish Tea Rings

½ cup soft butter
⅓ cup firmly packed brown sugar
1 egg yolk
½ tsp vanilla
1 cup all-purpose flour
1 egg white, lightly beaten
¾ cup very finely chopped blanched almonds
2 tbsp red currant jelly (see preserves section)

Cream the butter and sugar together till fluffy. Add the egg yolk and vanilla. Work in the flour, using your hands if necessary, until the dough is smooth. Shape the dough into 36 balls and dip into the egg white. Roll in the chopped almonds. Place on a greased cookie sheet. Make a well in each cookie, using a thimble.

Bake at 325 degrees for 5 minutes. Remake the wells if necessary and fill with jelly. Return to the oven for 8-10 minutes or until light golden.

1 cup soft butter
¼ cup icing sugar
1 tsp vanilla
¼ tsp almond extract
2 cups sifted all-purpose flour
¼ tsp cream of tartar
1 cup very finely chopped
  almonds
1 tbsp water
½ cup icing sugar, sifted

Almond Crescents

Cream the butter till light and fluffy. Gradually beat in the icing sugar and add the vanilla and almond extract. Sift together the flour and cream of tartar. Work into the creamed mixture along with the nuts. Sprinkle the water on the dough and, using your hands, blend the ingredients together to form a smooth dough.

Shape the dough into crescents, about 1 ½ tsp for each. Place on an ungreased baking sheet.

Bake at 300 degrees for 15 to 18 minutes or until lightly browned. Remove from the pan, and while still warm sprinkle with or roll in the ½ cup sifted icing sugar.

Yield: about 6 dozen.

⅓ cup butter
1 ½ cups firmly packed brown
  sugar
1 egg, separated
1 ¼ tsp vanilla
¾ cup sifted all-purpose flour
1 tsp baking powder
½ tsp salt
¾ cup chopped pecans

Rich Pecan Squares

Cream the butter until light and fluffy. Gradually beat in 1 cup of the brown sugar, the yolk of the egg, and 1 tsp of the vanilla, beating to make a smooth creamy batter. Sift together the flour, baking powder, and salt and stir into the creamed mixture, along with ½ cup of the chopped pecans. Spoon evenly into a greased 7" x 11" cake tin.

Beat the egg white till stiff but not dry. Beat in the rest of the sugar and the vanilla. Spread this topping over the batter. Sprinkle with the remaining ¼ cup chopped pecans. Bake at 325 degrees for 35-40 minutes or until the top is lightly browned and the mixture has come away from the sides.

Yield: 2 dozen squares.

3 tbsp butter
¼ cup molasses
2 tbsp water
1 cup sifted all-purpose flour
¼ tsp soda
1-2 tbsp ground ginger (2 tbsp makes them exceptionally snappy!)
¼ tsp ground cinnamon
¼ tsp freshly grated nutmeg
½ cup white sugar
⅛ tsp salt

Very Hot Ginger Snaps

Bring the butter, molasses, and water to the boil in a large saucepan. Stir to melt the butter. Cool.

Sift the dry ingredients together. Add to the molasses mixture. Incorporate into a ball. Cool at least 1 hour.

Divide the dough into 4 parts. Roll out each part very thin, ⅛", on a lightly floured board. Cut into desired shapes. The dough may appear initially to be too dry, but in fact works quite well. The cookies may be brushed with beaten egg white and sprinkled with sugar.

Bake 6 minutes at 350 degrees. Yield: five dozen 1 ½" cookies.

1 lb dates (the kind separated from each other, not the ones jammed together)
2 oz whole almonds
¾ cup icing sugar
½ cup ground almonds
3 tbsp soft butter
½ tsp vanilla, rose water, or almond extract
⅓ cup white sugar

Almond Stuffed Dates

Slit dates and remove stone. Place the whole almonds in a bowl, and cover with boiling water. Let stand 3-4 minutes or until the skins will slip off easily. Dry thoroughly before using. There should be about 50 of each.

Blend to a smooth paste the icing sugar, ground almonds, butter, and flavouring. Stuff each date with a small spoonful of the paste and push an almond into the paste, leaving about ¼ visible. Roll the dates in the white sugar. Pack in layers, separated by waxed paper in a container with a tight-fitting lid. Keep in a cool place.

Yield: about 1 ¾ lbs.

New Year's Buffet

Oyster Soup

Spiced Beef
Sliced Pork Tenderloins with Sage and Currant Stuffing
or
Mushroom and Nut Stuffing

Assortment of:
Green Tomato Pickle
Peach Chutney
Chili Sauce
Uncooked Chili Sauce
Icicle Pickles
Bread and Butter Pickles
Mustard Beans

Canadian Cheeses:
Wine-cured Cheddar
Oka
Limburger
Colby
Farmer's
Brick
St. Benoit
Ermite Blue

Whole Wheat Soda Bread
Nova Scotia Oatcakes

Fruit:
Russet Apples
Delicious Apples
Winter Pears

Mincemeat Pie
Lemon Curd Tarts

Suggested beverages:
cold ale or lager *or* chilled rosé *or* dry red wine

This buffet features two Canadian specialties: spiced beef and stuffed pork tenderloin. Spiced beef is part of the tradition of preserving meat by salting, spicing, and smoking. A good lean piece of beef is rubbed with spices and left to absorb the flavours for three weeks. Recipes for spicing the beef used to abound in cookbooks, and it was readily available at Christmas. Now only a few butchers who pride themselves in the old traditions still make it. Pork tenderloins can be stuffed with a nut and mushroom dressing or with currants and apples and served hot or cold. Both spiced beef and pork tenderloin are probably legacies from Irish settlers.

Oysters are at their peak in the winter, after they have spawned. In nineteenth-century cookbooks, "half a hundred" were frequently called for in stuffings and sauces, and stewed oysters were a feature of church socials. It may no longer be possible to enjoy them in such lavish quantities, but a few bowls of them poached in rich milk and sprinkled with cracker crumbs are easy to manage.

New Year's is an ideal time to serve an assortment of Canadian-made cheeses. Besides cheddar, there is the celebrated Oka made by Trappist monks in Oka, Quebec, a soft, almost buttery, cheese with a "distinctive" smell. The Benedictine monks of St. Benoit du Lac in Quebec make two other excellent cheeses, a mild blue called Ermite and a lovely cheese they have named St. Benoit. This latter is a creamy colour and has holes like Swiss cheese. It has a mild, sweet flavour with a delicate, nutty taste. Another soft cheese with an even more distinctive smell than Oka is Limburger, made in Baden, Ontario. It is not for the uninitiated. Colby, Brick, and Farmer's cheese are newly popular mild cheeses. All three are made from partly skimmed milk. They have an almost airy texture.

Except for the Limburger, allow all the cheeses to come to room temperature before serving. Keep the Limburger refrigerated in a screw-top jar till the last possible moment!

Recipes for the suggested pickles and relishes can be found in the preserves section at the end of the book.

5 cups milk
¼ cup finely rolled soda
   cracker crumbs
1 ½ tsp salt
dash of finely ground pepper
dash of nutmeg
4 tbsp butter
1 pint shucked oysters and
   their juice
2 tbsp finely chopped fresh
   chives or fresh parsley

Oyster Soup

Scald the milk over low heat. The milk is ready when it forms bubbles all around the side of the pot.

Add the cracker crumbs, salt, pepper, nutmeg, butter.

Drain the oysters. Add the juice to the milk.

When the butter has melted, add the oysters to the milk. Simmer the soup gently until the oysters plump up and begin to curl around the edges. This will take about 3 minutes. Be careful. If the oysters are cooked too long they will be tough; however, the soup must be hot enough.

Serve *immediately* sprinkled with the chopped parsley or chives. You may cut each oyster into 3-4 pieces if you like.

one 8-lb bottom round of beef,
   trimmed of all fat and bones

Marinade:
1 oz saltpeter
2 tbsp brown sugar
2 tsp ground cloves
2 tsp freshly grated nutmeg
2 tsp ground allspice
1 cup pickling salt
2 tbsp finely crushed dry bay
   leaves

Cooking:
1 tbsp ground cloves
1 tbsp ground allspice
1 cup water
piece of suet, 2-3 oz

Spiced Beef

Place beef on a soft absorbent cloth large enough to wrap around meat completely. An old tea towel is ideal.

Combine dry ingredients for marinade. Pour over the beef and rub well into the surface. Wrap the beef in the cloth and place in a crock or glass bowl, cover, and refrigerate. Turn beef daily, kneading spices into beef, without removing cloth. The beef and spices form their own liquid. Leave for at least 2 weeks; 3 weeks is better.

To cook, rinse beef in cold water. Dry. Combine the 1 tbsp cloves and the 1 tbsp allspice and dust over the meat. Place in a roasting pan and add water. Slice the suet and spread over the top of the meat. Cover tightly and roast at 300 degrees for 3 hours. Remove from the pan and while still hot pack beef into a bowl or crock. Cover with a plate and weigh down 24 hours till cold and well pressed. Slice thinly.

2 large tenderloins, ¾-1 lb each
  (close in size)
2 tbsp soft butter
1 tsp dry mustard
½ tsp freshly ground pepper
1 tsp salt

Sliced Pork Tenderloins with Sage and Currant Stuffing or Mushroom and Nut Stuffing

Wipe tenderloins, place skin side down on cutting board. Make a slit lengthwise almost through the middle of each tenderloin. Spread each loin apart and slit each side once in a similar manner. Pound the loins with a wooden mallet to about ¾" even thickness.

Spread the dressing over one loin, skin side down, and place the other loin skin side up on top of the first, forming a kind of sandwich. Put the narrow end of the top loin over the wide end of the bottom loin. This gives a more even roll of meat and dressing.

Skewer or sew the edges together. Combine the butter, mustard, and pepper into a paste and rub onto the loins. Loosely cover with foil.

Roast at 350 degrees 1 ¼ hours turning the pork over halfway through roasting. Baste periodically.

Uncover and roast another ½ hour, salting 15 minutes before the end of cooking time. Serve hot or cold in slices.

For a large buffet, buy 4 tenderloins. Stuff 1 pair with the sage and currant stuffing and the other pair with the mushroom and nut stuffing (see below).

2 tbsp butter
¼ cup finely chopped onions
¼ tsp salt
⅛ tsp freshly ground pepper
¼ tsp dried crumbled sage
1 ¼ cups coarse, stale, but not
  dry bread crumbs
⅓ cup currants
1 tbsp plum and raisin
  conserve (see preserves
  section)

Sage and Currant Stuffing

Melt the butter. Add the onions and seasonings. Sauté over medium heat 4-5 minutes or until the onions are transparent. Pour over the bread crumbs. Add the currants and conserve. Toss well to blend flavours.

Mushroom and Nut Stuffing

3 tbsp butter
2 tbsp finely chopped onions
¾ cup finely chopped
   mushrooms
½ tsp salt
¼ tsp freshly ground pepper
¼ tsp dried crushed thyme
1 ¼ cups coarse, stale, but not
   dry bread crumbs
2 tbsp finely chopped parsley
¼ cup chopped almonds,
   walnuts, or hazelnuts

Melt the butter and sauté the onions and mushrooms 4-5 minutes over medium heat. Add the salt, pepper, and thyme. Pour over the crumbs, parsley, and nuts. Toss thoroughly.

Whole Wheat Soda Bread

2 cups sifted all-purpose flour
1 tbsp white sugar
2 tsp soda
2 tsp salt
4 ½ cups whole wheat flour
2 ½ cups buttermilk or sour
   milk
2 tbsp sweet milk

Sift together flour, sugar, soda and salt. Place in a large bowl with the whole wheat flour. Mix thoroughly. Make a well in the centre and add the buttermilk. You may need to add more than 2 ½ cups. Mix enough to make a soft elastic dough. Knead it lightly into a ball in the bowl.

Turn out onto a greased baking sheet and pat into a circle 1 ½" thick. Mark an X ¼" deep with a floured knife. Brush surface with sweet milk.

Bake at 425 degrees for 25 minutes. Reduce heat to 350 degrees and continue baking 15 minutes more or until bread sounds hollow when tapped.

Remove from sheet and cool on a rack. It is best if left 4 hours before being sliced.

Nova Scotia Oakcakes

3 cups rolled oats (not instant)
3 cups sifted all-purpose flour
1 cup brown sugar
1 tsp soda
2 tsp salt
1 ½ cups shortening
⅔-¾ cup cold water

Combine oats, flour, sugar, soda and salt. Cut in the shortening with a pastry blender or 2 knives until the mixture is crumbly.

Using a fork, gradually add enough water for mixture to form a ball.

Roll out ⅜" thick on a lightly floured board. Cut into circles and place on a greased baking sheet.

Bake at 350 degrees for 15 minutes.

Yield: about 4 dozen cakes, depending upon size.

Mincemeat:
1 lb ground lean beef
1 lb fresh beef suet, shredded
   (2 cups)
2 cups dark brown sugar
2 cups sultana raisins
2 cups seeded raisins
2 cups currants
6 large apples, cored and
   grated
1 cup diced candied citron
   peel
1 ½ tsp salt
grated peel of 4 lemons
juice of 4 lemons
½ cup cider or apple juice
4 nutmegs, freshly grated (2
   tbsp)
3 tbsp ground cinnamon
2 tbsp ground coriander
½ cup dark rum
½ cup brandy

Pie:
sufficient pastry for a 2-crust 9"
   pie (see basic recipes)
3 ½ cups mincemeat
½ cup chopped apples
2 tbsp rum or brandy

Hot Mincemeat Pie

In a large preserving kettle, brown the ground beef thoroughly.

Add the rest of the ingredients, except the rum and brandy. Bring to the boil and cook 15 minutes. Stir constantly to prevent burning.

Remove from the heat. Stir the rum and brandy into the mincemeat.

Put into sterilized jars. Seal and store in a cool dry place.

Yield: 7 pints.

Line pie plate with pastry. Do not trim edges.

Combine mincemeat, apples, and rum.

Spoon into bottom crust, heaping filling towards the middle.

Roll out pastry for the top crust. Dampen the edges of the bottom crust. Place the top crust over the filling, pressing it around the edges. Trim around the edge of the pie plate. Flute. Slash 6-8 small steam holes in the top crust.

Bake at 450 degrees for 15 minutes. Reduce heat to 350 degrees and continue baking 30 minutes longer or until the crust is golden brown.

For Tarts:
Sufficient pastry for 2 ½ dozen tart shells and lids. Line tart shells with pastry. Fill ¾ full with mincemeat mixture. Cut out circles of pastry to fit over the mincemeat but not touch the edges. Place over the mincemeat. Bake at 450 degrees for 15 minutes, reduce heat to 350 degrees, and continue baking until the pastry is golden brown.

sufficient pastry for 2 ½-3 dozen
   tarts (see basic recipes)
6 eggs
2 cups white sugar
2 tbsp grated lemon rind
¾ cup lemon juice (3 lemons)
¾ cup melted butter
whipped cream (see basic
   recipes)
mint

Lemon Curd Tarts

Beat eggs until light and foamy. Add sugar, rind, juice, and butter. Place in a heavy-bottomed saucepan or in the top of a double boiler and cook over low heat until thickened, smooth, and like honey. Stir constantly. Cool.

Yield: about 3 dozen tarts.

To serve, spoon into baked, pricked tart shells. Top with sweetened whipped cream. A sprig of fresh mint or a sprinkle of crushed dried mint over the whipped cream is good.

Prime Ribs of Beef Dinner

Creamed Carrot Soup
or
Classic Potato Soup

Prime Ribs of Beef with Horse-radish and Mustard Sauce
Individual Yorkshire Puddings
Deluxe Cauliflower au Gratin

Mixed Green Salad with Ermite Blue Cheese Dressing

Old-fashioned Trifle

Suggested wine:
full-bodied red

Creamed soups are naturals for the winter. This potato soup is a somewhat refined version of the old rural standby and a close first cousin of vichyssoise. The fineness of all good soups depends on good stock, well-flavoured vegetables, lots of cream, and just the right amount of simmering.

Prime ribs of beef make the best roast of beef even though they don't come from the overpraised hind quarter. This roast has well-marbled lean, a protective layer of fat along one side, and flavoursome bones on the other. A slice of well-aged rib roast cooked rare, or at the most medium rare, is really splendid.

Cauliflower is one of the finest fall and winter vegetables. In this recipe it is cooked with a sauce and a thin layer of whipped cream and crumbs. Then it is broiled until it is crisp and golden brown on top and creamy underneath.

The dessert is old-fashioned trifle. Made in a glass bowl, the trifle's layers of sponge cake, custard, fruit, cream, and nuts can be well appreciated.

Creamed Carrot Soup

2 tbsp butter
1 medium onion, peeled and chopped fine
6 medium or 9 small carrots, scraped and diced evenly
5 tbsp flour
6 cups lightly salted chicken stock (see basic recipes)
1 tsp salt
1 bay leaf
¼ tsp dried crushed thyme
2 stalks parsley
½ tsp white sugar
1 cup milk
½ cup heavy cream
3 tbsp finely chopped parsley and chives, mixed

Melt the butter in a large, heavy-bottomed saucepan. Add the onions. Cook gently over low heat, covered, 1 minute. Add the carrots. Stir to coat the vegetables. Cover and continue cooking over low heat 15 minutes.

Stir in the flour. Cook 2-3 minutes without scorching. Heat the stock and add it gradually to the carrots, stirring constantly to prevent lumps. Add the salt, bay leaf, thyme, parsley, and sugar. Simmer uncovered for 15 minutes. The soup will be somewhat reduced and the flavour matured. Remove the bay leaf and parsley.

Scald the milk and cream. Add to the soup. Taste. Add more salt if desired.

Serve in bowls or in a tureen sprinkled with the chopped parsley and chives.

Classic Potato Soup

3 tbsp butter
1 ½ cups finely chopped onions (2 large onions)
4 cups potatoes peeled and cut in ½" cubes (5 medium potatoes)
1 tbsp flour
3 cups lightly salted chicken stock (see basic recipes)
1 bay leaf
6 stalks parsley
1 tsp salt
¼ tsp freshly ground pepper
3 cups light cream
salt
3 tbsp finely chopped parsley

Melt butter in a large saucepan. Add onions and cook over medium heat until onions are transparent but not browned, about 4-5 minutes. Add the potatoes, stirring well to coat with butter. Continue cooking gently for 5 minutes. Stir in the flour. Heat the chicken stock and add it to the vegetables with the bay leaf, parsley, 1 tsp salt, and pepper. Cover and simmer 25-30 minutes or until the potatoes are tender. Remove the bay leaf and parsley stalks. Press through a sieve or food mill or blend until smooth. Return to saucepan. (Traditionally the soup was not blended, but this makes it more elegant.)

Scald the cream and add to the soup. Taste. Add more salt if desired. Serve garnished with parsley.

one 6-lb prime rib roast of
  beef, first three ribs
2 cloves garlic
3 tbsp butter
1 tbsp dry mustard
½ tsp freshly ground pepper
1 tsp salt
¼ cup water or beef stock (see
  basic recipes)
salt and pepper

Prime Ribs of Beef with Horse-radish and Mustard Sauce

Cut the garlic cloves into 3-4 slivers. Poke the slivers into various nooks in the roast.

Combine the butter, mustard, and pepper. Smear this paste over the meat. Place the meat on a rack in an open roasting pan. Let it stand at least one hour at room temperature.

Roast uncovered at 350 degrees 15 minutes per pound for rare and 18 minutes per pound for medium rare, 20-25 minutes for well-done. For rare the thermometer registers between 130 and 140 degrees, for medium 140-150, and for well-done 150-170.

Remove from the oven. Sprinkle with salt. Place the roast on a preheated platter in a warm place for 25-30 minutes. The roast will not get cold and the meat will be easier to carve. This also allows time to bake the Yorkshire pudding (see below).

Remove the fat from the roasting pan. Pour the water or stock into the pan, work off all those delicious brown particles, season with salt and pepper, and add any pink juices that have come out of the roast. Serve in a preheated sauce boat.

¼ cup freshly grated
  horse-radish (if only bottled
  horse-radish is available,
  increase quantity to ⅓ cup
  and omit the vinegar and
  sugar)
1 tsp cider vinegar
½ tsp dry mustard
¼ tsp salt
½ tsp white sugar
½ cup whipped cream

Horse-radish and Mustard Sauce

Drain horse-radish thoroughly. Combine with the vinegar, mustard, salt, and sugar. Fold into the whipped cream just before serving.

2 eggs
1 cup milk
1 tbsp drippings from roast
1 cup unsifted all-purpose
   flour
¾ tsp salt

Yorkshire Pudding

Combine all ingredients in a bowl and beat until smooth with an electric mixer.

Pour into 12 greased muffin tins.

Bake at 425 degrees for 30 minutes. Remove from pans, and make a small incision in the bottom of each with a sharp knife to let steam escape. Serve around the roast.

Alternately: Bake in a greased 9″ x 9″ cake tin at 450 degrees for 15 minutes. Reduce heat to 350 degrees and bake another 10-15 minutes. Cut into squares and serve around the roast.

1 large cauliflower, about
   2 lbs
cold water
1 tsp salt
boiling water
¼ tsp salt
1 tsp lemon juice
¼ cup butter
¼ cup all-purpose flour
1 ½ cups hot cauliflower
   cooking liquid
1 cup light cream
¼ tsp mustard
⅛ tsp freshly ground pepper
1 cup grated old cheddar
   cheese
salt
3 tbsp butter
6 tbsp crisp bread crumbs
¼ cup heavy cream, whipped

Deluxe Cauliflower au Gratin

Break cauliflower into 16-18 large flowerets. Cover with cold water. Add 1 tsp salt. Soak 15 minutes. Drain and rinse.

Simmer flowerets uncovered in boiling water with ¼ tsp salt and lemon juice until tender, about 12 minutes. Drain, reserving 1 ½ cups cooking liquid.

Melt the ¼ cup of butter in a heavy-bottomed saucepan. Stir in the flour. Cook 3-4 minutes over medium heat. Gradually add the hot cauliflower liquid, stirring to prevent lumps. Stir in the cream, mustard, pepper, and cheddar cheese. Cook until cheese melts. Taste. Add more salt if necessary.

Melt the 3 tbsp butter, stir in the crumbs, and fry gently 3-4 minutes to brown lightly. Reserve.

Place the cauliflower in a greased, ovenproof casserole. Pour the sauce over it, spread on a thin layer of the whipped cream, and then sprinkle on the buttered crumbs.

Bake at 375 degrees for 20 minutes until top is golden and sauce bubbles around cauliflower.

1 head of lettuce, romaine,
  endive, Bibb, or chicory (a
  mixture is good)
½ green pepper
1 stalk celery
¼-½ 8″ cucumber
3-4 thin slices mild onion,
  Spanish or Bermuda
3 tbsp butter
⅔ cup cubed white homemade
  bread (see basic recipes)

Dressing:
6 tbsp olive oil
2 tbsp cider or wine vinegar, or
  lemon juice
1 tsp salt
½ tsp freshly ground pepper
¼ tsp dried crushed marjoram
  or ½ tsp fresh chopped
¼ cup crumbled Ermite blue
  cheese

Mixed Green Salad with Ermite Blue Cheese Dressing

Break the lettuce into bite-size pieces. Cut the green pepper into ¼″ strips and the celery into diagonal slices ¼″ thick. Peel and slice the cucumber. Combine all these vegetables and the onion slices in a large salad bowl, cover and chill.

Melt the butter over medium heat in a frying pan. When the butter has frothed up add the bread cubes and sauté gently until the cubes are golden brown and crisp but not burned. Remove and drain on paper towel. Cool. Combine all the ingredients for the dressing.

To serve, sprinkle the croutons onto the greens, pour on the dressing and toss well. Serve immediately.

---

1 sponge cake (see below)
½ cup sherry
1-1½ cups jam or jelly, currant
  and raspberry are favourites
  (fresh fruit, for example sliced
  strawberries or peaches or
  whole raspberries, would
  replace the jam in the
  summer)
1 making of rich custard (see
  below)
½ cup almonds, slivered and
  toasted (see basic recipes)
½ pint heavy cream
1 tsp sugar
pinch salt
½ tsp vanilla
½ cup toasted, slivered
  almonds (see basic recipes)

Old-fashioned Trifle

In a deep round glass bowl, put a layer of cake. Sprinkle with ¼ cup of the sherry. Spread half the jelly or jam, half the custard and the first ½ cup almonds over the layer.

Repeat with another layer of cake, the rest of the sherry, jam or jelly, and custard.

Cover and refrigerate for at least 1 hour.

Whip the cream. Add sugar, salt and vanilla. Spread the whipped cream over the custard. Decorate with the rest of the slivered almonds.

1 cup cake flour
⅛ tsp salt
3 eggs, separated
1 cup white sugar
¼ cup orange juice
¼ tsp grated orange rind

Sponge Cake for the Trifle

Sift the flour and salt together 4 times.

Beat the egg whites, adding ½ cup of the sugar slowly until the mixture is stiff.

Beat the egg yolks till they form a ribbon when a spoon is drawn out of them. Add the remaining ½ cup sugar.

Blend the white and yolk mixtures carefully. Add the orange juice and rind. Fold in the flour until just blended.

Spoon into an ungreased 9″ tube pan, or for the trifle, two 8″ ungreased layer tins. Run a knife across the cake through the batter 5-6 times.

Bake at 350 degrees for 35-40 minutes for the tube pan, 20-25 minutes for the layers. The cake should spring back when lightly touched.

Invert over a bottle if a tube, turn over racks if layers. Cool, loosen with a knife, remove from the pans.

2 cups milk
6 egg yolks
⅓ cup white sugar
¼ tsp salt
⅛ tsp vanilla or rose water

Custard for the Trifle

Scald the milk in the top of a double boiler over direct medium heat until little bubbles form around the edge. Beat the egg yolks and blend in the sugar and salt. Pour ½ cup of the hot milk into the yolks, stirring well. Stir back into the rest of the milk, and place over simmering water. Cook slowly, stirring constantly until the custard is thick enough to coat a spoon, 165 degrees. Remove the custard from the heat and stir 2-3 minutes as the custard cools. Strain through a sieve and add the flavouring.

Cool the custard, preferably over a large pan of cold water. Stir several times as it cools.

Baked Stuffed Lake Trout Dinner

Split Pea and Ham Soup

Baked Stuffed Lake Trout
Braised Celery Hearts

Marinated Beet Salad

Cranberry Ice
Classic Oatmeal Cookies

Suggested wine:
chilled white

There are three great inland fish for mid-winter eating, pickerel, whitefish, and lake trout. Even though all these fish are available in the summer, it is in the winter that they are fished commercially through the ice. Most of these fish come from lakes in the northern Prairie Provinces and the North West Territories. Whitefish is the most abundant of them, and accounts for a third of the value of all fish caught inland in Canada. However, both the pickerel and lake trout have a closer-textured flesh, which many people prefer. All three are excellent filled with savoury herbed dressing and baked.

Celery is not often eaten as a hot vegetable, but it is a shame to restrict it to the salad bowl. In this menu, the trimmed hearts are simmered in stock with finely chopped onion and carrot. Then they are drained and arranged on an open platter. The stock, thickened a little with flour and butter is poured over the hearts, and a sprinkle of parsley sets them off visually.

Salad need not always consist of leaves. Marinated beets for example, make a first-class Canadian winter salad.

Split Pea and Ham Soup

2 cups (1 lb) dried split peas
12 cups water
1 smoked ham bone plus any meat scraps
1 cup finely chopped onions (2 medium)
1 cup finely chopped carrots (2-3 medium)
½ cup chopped celery, stalk and leaves
¼ tsp ground cloves
½ tsp freshly ground pepper
1 bay leaf
salt

Combine the peas and water. Bring to the boil. Remove from the heat and let stand 1 hour. Skim any impurities from the top. Add the bone, vegetables, and seasonings but not the salt. Simmer uncovered about 2 hours or until the peas are tender.

Taste, add salt if necessary. Remove bone and bay leaf. Chop any meat from the bone back into the soup.

For a smooth soup, pass through a sieve or food mill or use a blender. Return to saucepan. Heat through. For better flavour, serve the following day.

Garnish with croutons (see fall grilled steak menu) or 1 tsp sour cream or 1 tsp lightly salted whipped cream on top of each bowl.

Baked Stuffed Lake Trout

2 cleaned, very fresh lake trout (or pickerel or whitefish), about 2 lbs each
juice and grated rind of ½ large lemon

Dressing:
4 ½ cups fine soft bread crumbs
6 tbsp butter
⅔ cup chopped green onions
½ tsp salt
¼ tsp freshly ground pepper
1 tbsp finely chopped parsley
1 tsp chopped fresh basil or ½ tsp dried crushed basil

Fish Coating:
¼ cup soft butter
1 tbsp flour
½ tsp salt
¼ tsp pepper
parsley
1 lemon, thinly sliced

Wipe the fish inside and out with a damp cloth. Sprinkle the cavities with about 1 tsp lemon juice. Reserve the rest of the juice.

To prepare the dressing, place the bread crumbs in a large bowl. Add the grated lemon rind.

Melt the butter in a frying pan over moderate heat. Sauté the onions until transparent, 3-4 minutes. Mix in the salt, pepper, parsley, and basil. Cook 2 minutes.

Pour the butter mixture over the crumbs and lemon rind. Toss well to blend the flavours. Divide the dressing into 2 parts. Stuff each fish with ½ the dressing. Close the sides together, press toothpicks through both sides, and lace up each fish with heavy thread.

Smear the fish all over with the soft butter. Lay in a large, shallow roasting pan. Sprinkle with the remaining lemon juice.

Bake for a total of about 30 minutes at 375 degrees (10 minutes per pound plus 10 extra minutes). Baste with accumulated pan juices after 10 minutes.

After the first 15 minutes of cooking, sprinkle each fish with the flour and the rest of the salt and pepper. Return the fish to the oven. Wait 5 minutes. Baste to set the crust. Return to oven for 10 minutes.

Remove fish to a heated platter. Take out the thread and toothpicks. Pour any pan juices around the fish.

Garnish with parsley and lemon slices. Serve immediately.

Braised Celery Hearts

6 celery hearts (large outer stalks of heads removed)
boiling water
½ cup green onions, chopped finely
½ cup carrots, chopped finely
1 cup chicken stock (see basic recipes)
½ tsp salt
¼ tsp freshly ground pepper
1 tbsp butter
1 tbsp flour
2 tbsp parsley, chopped finely

Split each head of celery in half lengthwise. Trim each off about 6"-7" from the base. Clean under running water.

Simmer the hearts for 10 minutes in boiling, unsalted water. Drain.

Lay the hearts in a single layer in a flat baking dish. Sprinkle them with the chopped onions and carrots. Pour on the stock and sprinkle lightly with salt and pepper. Cover the dish tightly and bake in a 350-degree oven 30 minutes or until the celery is tender.

Remove the celery to a warm platter. Combine the butter and flour to form a paste. Place the stock over a medium heat and gradually add the butter and flour paste to the stock, stirring to prevent lumps. Correct seasoning. Pour the sauce over the celery hearts. Garnish lavishly with the parsley.

Marinated Beet Salad

10 medium beets (about 1 ½ lbs or 2 bunches)
boiling water
½ tsp salt
3 tbsp cider vinegar
½ tsp salt
½ tsp freshly ground pepper
¼ tsp dry mustard
1 tsp white sugar
6 tbsp oil
1 tsp chopped fresh tarragon or ½ tsp dried crushed tarragon
12 thin slices of mild onion, separated into rings
⅔ cup thinly sliced celery

Simmer the beets until tender in the boiling water and ½ tsp salt, about 30-40 minutes. Peel and slice while still warm. There should be about 3 cups of sliced beets. Add the vinegar, salt, pepper, mustard, and sugar. Marinate 1 hour.

Just before serving, toss together with the oil and tarragon. Place in a glass serving dish layered with the onion rings and celery. Pour any remaining marinade over the top.

2 cups cranberries
¾ cup water
1 cup white sugar
1 ½ cups water
2 tbsp lemon juice
pinch of salt

Cranberry Ice

Cover and cook cranberries and ¾ cup water over medium heat until tender, about 10 minutes. Press through a sieve.

Combine sugar and 1 ½ cups water. Bring to boil and boil uncovered 6 minutes. Cool slightly. Combine with the cranberry purée, lemon juice, and salt. Pour into cake tins or freezer trays and freeze until it is mushy, 1-1 ½ hours. Transfer the mixture to a chilled bowl and beat with an electric mixer to break up the ice crystals. The mixture should be still quite frozen but rather smooth. Spoon into containers, cover well, and freeze until firm but preferably not solid.

1 cup butter
1 cup firmly packed brown
   sugar
1 egg
1 tsp vanilla
1 ½ cups sifted all-purpose
   flour
½ tsp salt
3 cups rolled oats
1 tsp soda
2 tbsp water
white sugar

Classic Oatmeal Cookies

Cream the butter till fluffy. Beat in the sugar and egg. Add the vanilla.

Sift together the flour and salt. Combine with the rolled oats and stir into the creamed mixture.

Stir the soda into the water. Mix into the dough.

Wrap in waxed paper and chill overnight.

Working with ½ the dough at a time, roll out very thin, ⅛", on a lightly floured board. Cut out cookies, sprinkle with white sugar, and place on greased baking sheets. Bake at 360 degrees about 7 minutes. The cookies should be crisp and golden. Cool on a rack. Store in a tin with a tight-fitting lid.

Yield: about 9 dozen 1 ½" cookies.

Two Winter Suppers

Here are two hearty suppers featuring exceptionally pleasing main courses that owe their excellence of flavour to long careful cooking. Every province (and probably every cook in every province) has a different version of baked beans. Quebec favours lots of molasses, chopped onions, and sometimes the inclusion of meats other than the traditional salt pork. In the Maritimes, a flavour of tomato is often found. The recipe given here is rich with molasses and includes both onions and tomatoes.

Steak and kidney pie, to be great, has to have a rich brown gravy and golden flaky crust. For people worried about kidneys, a presoak in salted water renders them particularly fine.

As these are virtually all-in-one dishes and rather smooth and rich as well, some of the chunkier crisp pickles are appropriate. Dilled pickles and pickled carrots contrast nicely with the beans, and pickled beets or mustard beans with the steak and kidney pie.

Recipes for the suggested pickles and relishes are found in the preserves section at the end of the book.

Canadian Baked Beans Supper

Canadian Baked Beans with Pork
Steamed Brown Bread
Dill Pickles and Pickled Carrots

Apple and Celery Salad

Toasted Almond Custard
Maple Sugar Cookies

Suggested beverage:
cold lager or ale *or* a robust red wine

2 cups navy beans
cold water
1 ½ tsp salt
½ lb salt pork
2 ½ cups stewed or canned
   tomatoes
1 cup finely chopped onions
1 ½ tsp dry mustard
¾ cup molasses
¼ tsp freshly ground pepper
¼ cup boiling water

Canadian Baked Beans with Pork

Pick over and wash beans. Cover generously with water (at least 2" above the beans) and soak overnight.

In the morning, add salt to undrained beans, bring slowly to the boiling point, and simmer gently until soft (about 30 minutes). Drain. Reserve liquid.

Cut salt pork into ¼" slices. Place half in the bottom of a bean pot. Add half the beans, the rest of the salt pork, half the tomatoes and onions, the remaining beans and the remaining tomatoes and onions.

Mix together the mustard, molasses, pepper, and water. Pour over the beans. Add any juice from the tomatoes and enough of the bean liquid to cover the beans plus ½ inch.

Cover pot tightly. Bake at 250 degrees for 8-9 hours. Add more reserved bean liquid or water as required.

Serve hot.

½ cup all-purpose flour,
   unsifted
1 tbsp soda
2 tsp salt
1 cup cornmeal
1 cup graham flour
½ cup molasses
2 cups buttermilk

Steamed Brown Bread

Sift together the all-purpose flour, soda, and salt. Combine with the cornmeal and graham flour.

Mix together the molasses and buttermilk. Stir into the dry ingredients.

Turn into a greased loaf tin 9" x 5". Grease a piece of aluminum foil and make a 1" pleat along the middle. Place over the loaf tin, leaving room for the bread to rise. Tie firmly around the edge.

Place on a rack in a large saucepan. Fill to ⅔ of the way up the loaf tin with boiling water. Cover and steam 2 hours, adding more boiling water when necessary to maintain the level.

For a crisp crust: after the loaf is cooked, place on a baking sheet and cook at 350 degrees until the exterior is crusty and dry, about 4 to 5 minutes.

Apple and Celery Salad

5 firm red apples, McIntosh are good (about 8 cups)
1 tbsp lemon juice
2 stalks tender celery (about 1 cup)
¾ cup freshly shelled walnut halves
½ cup raisins
1 cup mayonnaise (see basic recipes)
salt
lettuce leaves

Core and chop the apples. Sprinkle with the lemon juice. Add the rest of the ingredients and toss lightly to distribute the flavours. Taste. Add salt if desired. Spoon into a bowl lined with lettuce leaves.

Toasted Almond Custard

3 eggs
1 egg yolk
1 cup milk
1 cup light cream
½ cup white sugar
few grains of salt
1 tsp vanilla
⅓ cup slivered almonds

Beat eggs and yolk together, lightly. Set aside for the bubbles to subside.

Combine milk, cream, sugar and salt in a saucepan. Set over moderate heat. Stir only until the sugar dissolves. Bring to scalding point. Remove from heat. Add the vanilla.

Pour the milk in a steady stream into the eggs, stirring gently with a whisk. Strain into a shallow 1-quart, ovenproof dish. Set this dish in a larger pan. Pour a shallow bath of boiling water into the larger pan. Set in an oven at 350 degrees and bake approximately 30 minutes or until a knife inserted in the middle comes out clean. Ten minutes before the end of the baking time, sprinkle almonds around the edge of the custard. The almonds will toast as the rest of the custard sets.

Cool, refrigerate.

Maple Sugar Cookies

½ cup butter
½ cup white sugar
½ cup firmly packed grated maple sugar or brown sugar
1 egg
1 tsp vanilla
1 tbsp milk
2 cups sifted all-purpose flour
2 tsp baking powder
¼ tsp salt
¼ tsp freshly grated nutmeg

Cream butter till light and fluffy. Beat in the sugar and egg. Add the vanilla and milk.

Sift the flour together with the baking powder, salt, and nutmeg. Stir into the beaten mixture. Chill dough thoroughly.

Roll out ⅜" on a lightly floured board. Cut out with a floured cookie cutter.

(Or: form dough into a roll 2" in diameter, refrigerate overnight, and cut into thin slices.)

Bake at 375 degrees for 10 minutes or until delicately browned. Yield: 3-4 dozen.

Steak and Kidney Pie Supper

Steak and Kidney Pie with Glazed Flaky Pastry
Caraway Cabbage or Parsley Lemon Cabbage
Pickled Beets and Mustard Beans

Hot Gingerbread with Whipped Cream

Suggested beverage:
stout or ale *or* robust red wine

---

1 beef kidney (about ¾ lb)
1 ½ cups cold water
½ tsp salt
2 tbsp rendered fat from suet
2 tbsp butter
2 lbs chuck or round steak
¼ cup all-purpose flour
½ tsp salt
½ tsp freshly ground pepper
1 ½ cups sliced onions
½ cup sliced mushrooms
2 cups beef stock (see basic
   recipes)
1 bay leaf
2 stalks parsley
¼ tsp crushed dried summer
   savory
¼ tsp dry mustard
¼ tsp freshly ground pepper
salt to taste
flour for thickening
pie crust to cover (see basic
   recipes)
1 egg white, lightly beaten

Steak and Kidney Pie with Glazed Flaky Pastry

Split kidney, remove the suet, soak in cold water and ½ tsp salt for 1 hour. Dry kidney, cut into ½" pieces.

Render suet over medium heat in a large, thick-bottomed saucepan. Have butter handy.

Cut steak into 1" cubes. Combine flour, ½ tsp salt, and ½ tsp pepper in a paper bag. Shake the steak, a few pieces at a time, and then the kidney in this seasoned flour. Brown the steak in 4 lots, remove, and reserve. Brown the kidney. Add the butter as needed. Remove kidney. Add onions and mushrooms. Sauté 3-4 minutes or until the onions are barely transparent. Put the meat back into the pot. Add the stock, bay leaf, parsley, summer savory, mustard, and ¼ tsp pepper.

Bring to the boil, stirring well all the time. Cover, reduce heat, and simmer 1-1 ½ hours or until the meat is tender. Stir from time to time.

Taste, add salt if necessary. If the liquid is too thin, thicken with a little flour and water paste. Remove the bay leaf.

Place in a greased casserole. Cover with a flaky pastry. Make a few steam holes and pinch the pastry to the edge of the casserole. Brush the top with egg white.

Bake at 450 degrees for 10 minutes. Reduce the heat to 375 degrees and continue baking another 15 minutes or until the pastry is golden brown and the beef and kidney mixture is bubbling hot.

Caraway Cabbage

1 tbsp butter
8 cups shredded cabbage (1 medium cabbage)
1 tsp salt
1 clove garlic, minced
1½ tsp caraway seed
1 tsp brown sugar
1½ tbsp cider vinegar
½ cup sour cream

Melt the butter in a large, heavy-bottomed saucepan. Add the cabbage, salt, and garlic. Toss together. Cover tightly and cook over low heat until tender, about 10 minutes.

Add the rest of the ingredients. Stir well to coat all the cabbage. Heat through. Serve immediately.

Parsley Lemon Cabbage

¼ cup butter
8 cups shredded cabbage (1 medium cabbage)
1 tsp salt
½ tsp freshly ground pepper
2 tsp lemon juice
2 tbsp finely chopped parsley

Melt the butter in a heavy-bottomed saucepan. Add the cabbage, salt, pepper, and lemon juice. Toss to coat the cabbage. Cover and cook over medium heat until just tender, 5-6 minutes. Add the parsley, toss, and serve.

Hot Gingerbread with Whipped Cream

½ cup shortening
½ cup white sugar
1 egg
1 cup molasses
2½ cups sifted all-purpose flour
1½ tsp soda
½ tsp salt
1 tsp ground ginger
1 tsp ground cinnamon
½ tsp ground cloves
1 cup boiling water
whipped cream (see basic recipes)

Cream the shortening till light and fluffy. Beat in the sugar. Add the egg and beat well. Stir in the molasses.

Sift together the flour, soda, salt, and spices.

Add the dry ingredients in 3 parts alternately with the water in 2 parts to the creamed mixture. Start and end with the dry ingredients.

Pour into a well-greased 9″ x 9″ cake tin. Bake 50-60 minutes at 350 degrees. Cool in tin 5-10 minutes, cut into squares, and serve with whipped cream.

Preserves

The jams, pickles, and other preserves in this section are recommended condiments for the menus in the book. Hopefully, they may spark an interest in the sadly waning art of home preserving. They are alphabetized for convenience in locating them from the references in the menus.

Some Notes on Preserving

Wash jars, sealers, and lids in hot soapy water. Rinse thoroughly. The easiest way to sterilize jars is to set the jars on a rack in the oven preheated to 225 degrees and leave them 10 minutes. Use them from the oven, allowing them to cool slightly before filling them.

To seal jars for jam, jelly, conserve, and marmalade, fill the hot sterilized jars to within ¼" of the top. Take care not to dribble any jam on the inside of the jar above the jam level. Cool the jam slightly, unless otherwise directed, then pour a thin layer of melted paraffin wax over the jam. Tilt and rotate the jar as the wax is being poured. This ensures a perfect seal right to the edges. Let cool completely. Then complete the seal with another thin layer of melted paraffin wax. Tilt and rotate the jar as you did before. Cover the jars and store in a cool dry place. Once the jar is opened for use, it should be refrigerated.

Sealers and glass and metal screw tops should be sterilized in the same way as the jars. Rubber rings and lids with the rubber ring attached to the lid should never be re-used. Dip rings and lids briefly in boiling water before using. Be sure to fill sealers right up to the top unless otherwise directed.

Apple Butter

6 cups apple cider
5 lb apples (Tolman Sweets or Snow Apples are preferable but the popular McIntosh and Spies make good butter)
sugar
1 tsp ground cinnamon
¼ tsp ground allspice
¼ tsp ground cloves
¼ tsp freshly grated nutmeg

Pour the cider into a heavy-bottomed saucepan, place over high heat, and reduce the cider to half (3 cups). Reduce heat to medium.

Wash apples, quarter, remove blossom and stem ends. Slice and add to the cider. Cook uncovered until the apples are soft. Stir and mash during the cooking period. Press through a sieve or put through a food mill. Measure the pulp. Taste. Add ¼ cup of sugar per cup of pulp if the apples are very sweet, up to ½ cup sugar per cup of pulp for very sour apples. Add spices and cook over low heat until thick and dark brown, stirring frequently to prevent scorching. This may take up to 4 or 5 hours for the dark rich apple butter. Pack into hot sterilized jars. Seal with melted paraffin wax.

Yield: four or five 8-oz jars.

Black Currant Jelly

2 quarts stemmed black currants
water
4 cups white sugar

Measure currants into a preserving kettle. Add an equal quantity of water. Cover and simmer until the fruit is soft (10-15 minutes). Crush periodically with a potato masher.

Pour into a jelly bag and let the juice drain out overnight.

Measure out 4 cups of the juice. Place in

preserving kettle. Bring to the boil. Boil 3 minutes. Add 4 cups sugar. Return to the boil and continue cooking over high heat until the jelly sheets, about 5 minutes (see glossary).

Remove from the heat immediately. Rest 1 minute. Skim with a metal spoon. Pour into sterilized jars. Seal.

Yield: about six 6-oz jars for each 4 cups juice.

Brandied Cherries

2 quarts perfect sweet black cherries (Bing), about 2 ½ lbs
¾ cup white sugar
3 ½-4 cups brandy

Wash cherries. Dry on paper towel.

Cut off half the stem and prick each cherry with a needle.

Place cherries and 3 tbsp of the sugar in layers in four cold sterilized jars. Fill jars with brandy. Seal tightly. Shake gently to dissolve the sugar. Turn the sealers over periodically as the fruit matures. Leave 2 months before eating. Excellent with vanilla ice cream, or on their own with after-dinner coffee.

Yield: 4 pints.

Bread and Butter Pickles

10 cups sliced young cucumbers, about 1" in diameter
10 small onions
1 sweet red pepper
7 tbsp pickling salt
3-4 trays ice cubes
2 ¼ cups white wine vinegar
4 cups white sugar
1 tbsp mustard seed
1 tbsp celery seed
1 tsp freshly ground pepper

Place the cucumbers in a 2-gallon crock.

Slice the onions. Cut the pepper into rings or strips. Place both in the crock, add the salt, and cover with a thick layer of ice cubes. Let stand overnight.

Drain thoroughly.

Combine the rest of the ingredients, bring to the boil, and add the vegetables. Simmer 2-5 minutes on low heat, just long enough to heat the vegetables through. Pack immediately into hot sterilized jars. Seal.

Yield: about 6 pints.

Chili Sauce

30 large, ripe tomatoes
8 medium onions
3 sweet green peppers
2 sweet red peppers
¼ hot red pepper
2 cups chopped celery
3 cups cider vinegar
3 tbsp pickling salt
2-2 ½ cups firmly packed brown sugar
1 tsp freshly ground pepper
1 tsp ground ginger
1 tsp ground cinnamon
1 tsp ground allspice
1 tsp ground cloves
1 tsp freshly grated nutmeg
1 tsp celery seed

Scald the tomatoes with boiling water. Skin and chop them coarsely into a large preserving pot.

Peel and chop the onions medium-fine.

Remove the membrane and seeds from the sweet peppers. Chop medium-fine.

Very carefully chop the hot red pepper. Wash your hands immediately and don't touch your eyes or mouth.

Add the onions, peppers, celery, vinegar, salt, sugar, and spices to the tomatoes in the preserving pot.

Bring to the boil, reduce heat and simmer uncovered until thickened, about 2 ½-3 hours. Stir frequently to avoid scorching.

Pour into hot sterilized jars. Seal.

Yield: approximately 8 pints.

Concord Grape Jelly

3 quarts Concord grapes
½ cup water
7 cups sugar
½ bottle liquid pectin

Stem grapes. Crush thoroughly in a saucepan. Add the water. Cover. Bring to the boil. Reduce heat and simmer 10 minutes.

Place pulp in a jelly bag. Squeeze out juice.

Measure out 4 cups of juice. Combine with the sugar in a preserving kettle. Stir very well to dissolve the sugar. Place over high heat. Bring to the boil, stirring constantly. Stir in pectin. Bring to a full rolling boil. Boil hard 1 minute, stirring constantly. Remove from the heat. Remove scum with a metal spoon. Pour carefully into hot sterilized glasses. Seal immediately with melted paraffin wax.

Yield: eight-ten 6-oz jars.

Dilled Bean Sticks

3 lbs green beans
1 cup chopped fresh dill
2 cloves garlic, peeled and halved
2 cups water
2 cups white wine vinegar
¼ cup pickling salt
4 tsp sugar
½ tsp cayenne pepper

Remove tips from the beans and leave whole. Boil until crisp-tender, about 8-10 minutes.

Plunge into ice water quickly. Pack upright in sterilized pint jars.

Divide the dill and garlic among the jars.

Heat remaining ingredients together and add to the bean jars. Seal and store 1 month before using.

Yield: about 4 pints.

Dill Pickles

4 lbs slim pickling cucumbers, 4"-5" long. *Must be very fresh.*
6 cloves garlic
6 dill heads, fresh and abundant
3 cups water
3 cups white wine vinegar
6 tbsp pickling salt

Wash, wipe, and dry cucumbers.

Pack 6 pint sealers with the cucumbers. Add one good-sized dill head and one clove garlic to each pint.

Heat the water, vinegar, and pickling salt to boiling point.

Pour vinegar solution over the cucumbers, filling the jars to within ½" of the top.

Seal jars and immerse up to their necks on a rack in boiling water. Leave about 10 minutes or until the cucumbers begin to change colour.

Remove from the water. Cool and store in a cool, dry place for about 1 month before using.

N.B. This recipe will succeed only if fresh cucumbers are used.

Ginger Pear Marmalade

10 cups sliced firm pears (4 lbs, 10 large pears)
6 cups white sugar
2 lemons
½ cup sliced peeled fresh green ginger (3 oz)

Place the sliced pears and sugar in a large

preserving kettle.

Peel the zest off the lemons, and sliver finely. Juice the lemons. Add these ingredients and the ginger to the pears. Stir well, cover and leave overnight.

The next day, uncover, bring to the boil, reduce heat and stirring frequently, simmer gently 40-45 minutes or until the marmalade is thick and the fruit transparent. Pour into hot sterilized jars. Seal with melted paraffin wax.

Yield: about six 8-oz jars.

Green Tomato Pickle

4 quarts green tomatoes
4 large onions, peeled
4 sweet red peppers
¾ cup pickling salt
5 cups cider vinegar
5 cups white sugar
1 tsp freshly ground pepper
1 tsp mustard seed
1 tsp celery seed
1 tsp ground cloves
1 tsp ground allspice
1 tsp ground cinnamon

Slice the tomatoes and onions thinly. Remove membranes and seeds from peppers. Cut the peppers into rings or strips. Sprinkle the salt over the vegetables in layers. Let stand overnight. Drain the vegetables, rinse thoroughly in cold water, drain well again.

Combine the rest of the ingredients together in a large preserving kettle. Bring to the boil. Add the vegetables. Return to the boil and cook 30 minutes, stirring frequently to prevent sticking. Pack into hot sterilized jars and seal.

Yield: about 6-8 pints.

Icicle Pickles (11 Day Pickles)

one 6-quart basket of fresh 3"-4" cucumbers
2 cups pickling salt
1 gallon boiling water (20 cups)
boiling water
1 tbsp powdered alum
boiling water
12 ½ cups cider vinegar
16 cups white sugar
3 tbsp whole mixed pickling spice

First day: wash, dry, and cut cucumbers in half, lengthwise. Put in a crock. Dissolve the salt in the gallon of water and cover the cucumbers. Add more brine in the same proportions if necessary. Let stand 4 days. The brine will ferment.

Fifth day: drain brine from pickles and cover with clear boiling water. Let stand 24 hours.

Sixth day: drain. Dissolve alum in enough boiling water to cover the cucumbers. Pour over the cucumbers and let stand 24 hours.

Seventh day: drain. Combine the cider vinegar, 8 cups of the sugar, and whole pickling spice. Heat to boiling point and pour over the cucumbers. Let stand 24 hours.

Eighth day: drain syrup from the cucumbers. Heat to the boiling point. Dissolve 2 cups of the remaining sugar in the syrup. Pour over the cucumbers.

Ninth day and tenth day: repeat eighth day.

Eleventh day: drain syrup. Place cucumbers in hot sterilized jars. Heat syrup to boiling point. Add the last 2 cups of sugar. Pour syrup over pickles in jars, straining out the spices. Seal.

Yield: about 6 quarts.

Indian Pickles

3-4 quarts small firm cucumbers 2" long
1 quart small onions
1 medium head cauliflower
7 ½ cups white wine vinegar

2 oz whole mustard seed
three 1" pieces of dried ginger
4 pieces of chili pepper ½"-¾" long
2 tbsp turmeric
¼ cup mustard seed
2 tbsp powdered mustard
1 ½ tsp freshly ground pepper
5 tbsp pickling salt
4 cloves garlic

Wipe, but do not wash the cucumbers. Peel the onions. Break the cauliflower into flowerets about 1 ½". Place all three vegetables into a 2-gallon crock.

Boil all the other ingredients except the garlic together uncovered for 15 minutes. Add the garlic. Cool.

Pour the liquid over the vegetables. Cover with a plate. Weight down the plate so that all the vegetables are immersed.

The vegetables should be ready in about 6 weeks. You may add more vegetables any time. These pickles keep well. They are very sour.

Makes 1 gallon.

Mint-Apple Jelly

8 medium-large tart apples
cold water
3 cups white sugar
1 cup mint leaves, lightly packed

Remove stems and blossom ends from the apples. Cut into slices. Place in a heavy-bottomed preserving kettle. Add enough water to cover the fruit. Cover and cook over medium heat until apples are tender, about 15-20 minutes. Put apples and juice in a jelly bag and let drip overnight.

Measure out 4 cups of this juice and place in the preserving kettle. Add the sugar and mint leaves. Crush the leaves gently with a fork. Bring to the boil and boil hard until jelly sheets (see glossary). Strain out mint. Remove scum with metal spoon. Pour jelly into hot sterilized jars. Seal with melted paraffin wax.

Yield: four 8-oz jars.

Mustard Beans

3 lbs mixed yellow and green beans (about 4 quarts)
boiling water
1 tsp salt
1 ½ tsp ground turmeric
½ cup dry mustard
½ cup all-purpose flour
1 ½ tsp salt
2 cups firmly packed brown sugar
1 ½ cups cold water
3 cups cider vinegar
4 tsp celery seed
2 tsp mustard seed

Remove tips from the beans. Leave whole. Drop into rapidly boiling water with the 1 tsp salt. Cover and cook 8-9 minutes. Do not overcook. The beans should still be crisp. Drain.

In the meantime, combine the turmeric, mustard, flour, 1 ½ tsp salt, and brown sugar. Work to a smooth paste with the cold water.

Bring to the boil the vinegar, celery seed, and mustard seed. Stir ½ cup of the hot vinegar into the mustard mixture. Gradually add the mustard mixture into the rest of the hot vinegar, stirring constantly. Cook 5 minutes, until the sauce is smooth and thickened. Add the beans, bring back to the boil, reduce heat, and simmer 4-5 minutes or until the beans are just tender. Pour into hot sterilized jars. Seal.

Yield: about 4 pints.

Peach Chutney

7 lbs peaches, peeled and chopped
4 cups chopped onions
4 cups sultana raisins
6 cups firmly packed brown sugar
4 cups cider vinegar
1 tsp curry powder
1 tsp turmeric
1 tsp ground cinnamon
1 tbsp mustard seed
1 tbsp salt
¼ tsp cayenne pepper
1 tsp ground coriander
1 tsp ground cumin
½ tsp ground cardamom

Combine all ingredients in large preserving kettle. Bring to a boil, reduce heat, and simmer uncovered about 1 ½ to 2 hours. The chutney should be thick and dark golden colour.

Pour into hot sterilized jars and seal. Makes 9-10 pints.

Pickled Beets

40-50 small whole beets 1"-1 ½" diameter (one 6-quart basket)
2 tbsp salt
water
2 cups cider vinegar
2 cups beet water
1 cup firmly packed brown sugar
1 tbsp mixed pickling spice

Scrub but do not peel beets. Cut off the tops 1" from beet. Boil in salted water until tender, 20-25 minutes. Drain, reserving 2 cups of the beet water. Cool under cold water until you can handle them to remove the skins. Put in cold sterilized jars. Cool under cold water until you can handle them to remove the skins. Put in cold sterilized jars.

Meanwhile, boil for 5 minutes the vinegar, beet water, brown sugar, and mixed pickling spice. Pour the syrup over the beets almost to overflowing. Seal.

Yield: 4-5 pints.

Do not use for 3 weeks to allow the flavour to permeate the beets.

Pickled Carrots

2 ½ lbs small young carrots (about 2 quarts)
boiling water
1 strip lemon peel
3 cups white wine vinegar
1 cup white sugar
3 tbsp mixed pickling spice

Scrape the carrots. Cover with boiling water, add the lemon peel, and cook over moderate heat 7 minutes, or until half cooked. Drain, reserving ½ cup of the cooking liquid.

Combine the ½ cup cooking liquid with the vinegar, sugar, and spices. Bring to the boil. Boil gently 10 minutes. Add the carrots and cook 4 minutes or until just tender. Pack the carrots upright into hot sterilized jars, cover with pickling liquid, and seal.

Yield: about 3 pints.

Pickled Onions

2 quarts small white onions (3 lbs)
boiling water
cold water
¾ cup pickling salt
8 cups boiling water
cold water
4 cups white wine vinegar
1 cup white sugar
one 3" stick cinnamon, broken into pieces

Cover the onions with boiling water, let stand 3

minutes, drain, and cover again with cold water. Peel and put into a crock.

Dissolve the salt in the 8 cups boiling water, pour over the onions, and let stand overnight. Drain, rinse thoroughly with cold water, and drain again.

Bring the vinegar, sugar, and cinnamon to the boil. Boil 5 minutes, add the onions, and return to the boil. Remove from the heat and pack the onions and cinnamon immediately into hot sterilized jars. Cover with the pickling liquid and seal. Leave about 2 months before eating.

Yield: about 4 pints.

Pineapple-Rhubarb Conserve

8 cups pink rhubarb cut in ½″ pieces
2 cups very finely chopped pineapple (¼″ cubes)
4 cups white sugar

Combine rhubarb and pineapple in a heavy-bottomed preserving pan. Place over low heat until juice forms, about 20 minutes. Stir frequently to prevent burning.

Bring the fruit to the boil and boil uncovered 15 minutes, continuing to stir almost constantly, as the mixture is very thick.

Add sugar, stir in well, return to the boil, and continue boiling over moderate heat 25 minutes or until thick, clear, and at the jam stage (see glossary). Stir frequently during cooking.

Pour into hot sterilized jars, cool slightly, and seal with melted paraffin wax.

Yield: six 8-oz jars.

Platter Strawberry Jam

1 quart box strawberries (leave whole)
3 ½ cups white sugar

Hull and wash berries. Combine berries and

sugar in a heavy-bottomed preserving kettle. Stir gently.

Cook over a low heat until the sugar has melted, about 10 minutes.

Boil rapidly for 10 minutes, watching and stirring to prevent burning. Skim with a metal spoon.

Pour into a large platter, leave 24 hours. Bottle in cold sterilized jars and seal with melted paraffin wax.

Yield: four 8-oz jars.

Plum and Raisin Conserve

6 lbs plums (Lombards or prune plums)
4 large oranges
2 lbs raisins
12 cups sugar
2 cups walnut halves

Pit and quarter the plums. Cut the oranges into quarters, remove seeds and put through the medium blade of a food grinder. Combine the plums, oranges, raisins, and sugar in a large preserving kettle. Simmer 2 ½ hours or until quite thick and jelly-like. Add the walnuts, heat through, and pour into hot sterilized jars. Seal with melted paraffin wax.

Yield: about eight 8-oz jars.

Pumpkin Marmalade

one 5-lb pumpkin (16 cups diced)
3 lemons
1 orange
8 cups white sugar
1 cup water
¼ cup brandy

Peel pumpkin. Dice quite fine. Place in a large, heavy-bottomed preserving kettle.

Slice citrus fruit very thin. Remove seeds. Add

the fruit and sugar to pumpkin. Stir and leave overnight.

Place over medium heat. Add water. Simmer for 2 ½ hours or until thick. Stir in brandy. Pour into hot sterilized jars and seal with melted paraffin wax.

Yield: about twelve 8-oz jars.

Raspberry Vinegar

2 quarts raspberries
2 cups white wine vinegar
sugar

Combine raspberries and vinegar in a glass bowl or earthenware crock. Cover with a cloth and tie up well to keep out insects. Let stand for 4 days. Drain into a jelly bag and let drip overnight into a glass container. The next day measure the juice. There should be about 3 cups. Place in a saucepan and add 1 cup sugar for each cup of juice. Bring to the boil. Boil 20 minutes.

Pour into hot, sterilized sealers or bottles. Seal. Yield: about 2 pints.

To serve, place 3-4 ice cubes in a glass. Pour in 2 oz raspberry vinegar and fill up with 8 oz cold water or soda water.

Red Currant Jelly

8 cups stemmed red currants (about 2 quarts)
4 cups water
4 cups sugar

Combine red currants and water in a saucepan. Crush with a potato masher. Cover. Simmer 10-15 minutes or until the fruit is tender. Mash once or twice to encourage the formation of juice. Pour into a jelly bag and let drain overnight.

The next day, measure out 4 cups of juice and place in a preserving kettle. Bring to the boil.

Boil 3 minutes. Add 4 cups sugar and boil until the jelly sheets (see glossary). Remove from the heat. Remove scum with a metal spoon, let rest 1 minute. Pour into hot sterilized jars. When practically set, seal with melted paraffin wax.

Yield: six 6-oz jars from 4 cups of juice.

Ridgetown Corn Relish

12 cobs corn
1 quart cucumbers
6 sweet green peppers
1 sweet red pepper
1 quart red or green tomatoes
1 quart onions
5 cups white sugar
5 cups vinegar, cider, or white wine
1 tbsp celery seed
1 tbsp dry mustard
½ tbsp ground turmeric
1 tbsp salt

Cut kernels off cobs. Reserve. Put the cucumbers, peppers, tomatoes, and onions through the coarse blade of a grinder. Combine all the vegetables except the corn with the rest of the ingredients. Boil 1 hour over moderate heat. Add the corn. Boil 20 minutes. Pour into sterilized jars. Seal.

Yield: about 7 pints.

Royal Strawberry Acid

3 pints ripe strawberries
3 tbsp citric acid
3 cups cold water
3 ¾ cups white sugar

Slice the berries into a large bowl, add the citric acid and water, cover lightly, and leave 24 hours.

Bring to the boil in a saucepan, add the sugar,

return to the boil, and boil 3 minutes. Strain into hot sterilized sealers or bottles. Yield: about 1 quart.

To serve, pour 3 oz into a large glass, add 3-4 ice cubes, and fill up with about 8 oz cold water or soda water. Stir. Add a perfect unhulled berry to each glass.

Seville Orange Marmalade

5 Seville oranges
1 large sweet orange
2 lemons
10 cups water
8 cups white sugar
2 oz brandy

Slice the fruit very thinly. Remove the pips and place in a small bowl. Cover the fruit with 9 cups of the water and the pips with 1 cup. Leave 24-36 hours.

Place the fruit and water in a preserving kettle. Bring to the boil, reduce heat, and cook at a bare simmer for 3 hours. Add the sugar. Stir to dissolve. Using a sieve, drain the juice from the pips into the oranges by spooning juice from the kettle over the pips until they are no longer slippery. Bring the mixture to the boil. Boil about 1 hour or until it reaches the jam stage (see glossary). Stir in the brandy. Pour into hot sterilized jars. Seal with melted paraffin wax.

Yield: about eight 8-oz jars.

Spiced Crab Apples

2 ½ quarts rosy red crab apples
3 cups white sugar
2 cups cider vinegar
2 cups water
1 tbsp whole cloves
1 tbsp whole allspice

one 3" stick cinnamon
1 piece of dried ginger 1" long

Wash the crab apples. Leave on the stems but remove the blossom ends. Prick each apple several times with a fork.

Combine the sugar, cider vinegar, water, and spices in a preserving kettle. Bring to the boil and add the apples. Reduce heat. Simmer gently until the apples are tender but not broken, about 10 minutes.

Pack the apples in sterilized jars. Heat up the syrup to boiling and pour over the apples, filling the jars almost to overflowing. Seal immediately.

Yield: 4 pints.

Spiced Pears

4 lbs small hard pears
boiling water
five 2" pieces of cinnamon stick
1 tbsp whole cloves
1 tbsp whole allspice
4 ½ cups white sugar
2 cups cider vinegar

Peel the pears but leave on the stems if possible.

Simmer the pears 10 minutes in boiling water to cover. Drain off all the water except 1 cup.

Combine the spices, sugar, vinegar, and 1 cup pear water. Bring to the boil and let boil 5 minutes. Add the pears, cover, and cook over medium heat for 10-15 minutes or until the pears are transparent and tender.

Let stand overnight.

Reheat the pears and liquid to the boiling point. Pack the pears into hot sterilized jars. Boil up the liquid and pour it over the pears. Fill the jars to the top. Seal.

Yield: 4 pints.

Spiced Red Currant Jelly

4 cups red currants, washed
2 cups water
one 3" piece of cinnamon
1 dozen whole cloves
½ cup cider vinegar
7 cups white sugar
½ bottle liquid pectin

Combine the currants, water, cinnamon, and cloves in a heavy-bottomed preserving kettle. Crush with a potato masher. Cover and cook together 10 minutes, crushing 2-3 times to extract all the juice.

Pour the cooked fruit into a moistened jelly bag and let drip overnight. For a clear jelly, do not squeeze the bag.

Measure out 3 ½ cups juice into a large preserving kettle. Add the vinegar and sugar, stirring well to dissolve the sugar. Place the kettle on a very high heat, bring to a full rolling boil, and boil hard 1 minute exactly. Remove from the heat and stir in pectin. Skim off any foam, using a metal spoon. Pour into sterilized jars and seal with melted paraffin wax.

Yield: ten 8-oz jars.

Transparent Spiced Apples

2 cups white sugar
1 ½ cups cider vinegar
½ cup water
1 stick cinnamon broken into several pieces
1 tsp whole cloves
1 tsp whole allspice
1 tbsp grated fresh ginger root or ¾ tsp dry ground ginger
12 drops of red food colouring (more optional)
2 lbs Northern Spies (5-6 medium apples)

Combine sugar, vinegar, water, spices, and food colouring in a heavy-bottomed preserving kettle. Bring to the boil over high heat. Boil hard for 5 minutes. Reduce heat to medium.

Peel and core the apples. Divide each one into 8 pieces and poach these pieces in the simmering syrup until they are transparent but still holding their shape. Arrange around a meat platter.

Basic Recipes

These recipes are frequently called for in the menus in this book. They are all worth mastering as excellent, standard ingredients of good cooking in general. They are in alphabetical order.

Beef Stock

4-5 lbs of beef bones cut into 2″-3″ pieces
1 lb veal bones cut into 2″-3″ pieces
3 large carrots, sliced
2 celery stalks, chopped
2 large unpeeled onions, sliced
1 clove garlic
1 tsp dried crushed thyme or 2 tsp chopped
    fresh thyme
1 bay leaf
2 whole cloves
4 stalks parsley
2 tsp salt
8 peppercorns, crushed
3 tomatoes
1 leek, green part only, chopped
1 cup dry wine, red or white
20 cups cold water

Place the bones in a large open roasting pan. Add the carrots, celery, and onions. Roast at 450 degrees 3″ from the bottom of the oven for 15 minutes or until they are browned.

Place the bones and vegetables into a large stock pot. Add the rest of the ingredients. Bring to the boil. Reduce heat. Carefully skim off fat and scum. Gently simmer the stock, 5-6 hours, until it is reduced and well flavoured. Strain through a coarse sieve and then through a rinsed cheesecloth. Cool quickly. This stock can be used in soups such as the clear tomato soup or can be made into consommé. It can also be frozen and used for sauces or gravies. Take into account that the stock is lightly salted.

Yield: about 2 quarts.

Boiled Dressing

½ cup sugar
½ tsp salt
1 tsp dry mustard
½ cup vinegar

2 eggs, well beaten
1 tbsp butter

Combine sugar, salt, and mustard in the top of a double boiler. Add vinegar. Stir to combine. Add well-beaten eggs. Place over moderately boiling water. Stir until the mixture is creamy—about the consistency of custard. Beat in the butter. Cool. This dressing may be stored, covered, in the refrigerator, and will keep up to two weeks.

Chicken Stock

4 lbs of chicken backs, necks, wing tips
2 onions (1 cup), coarsely chopped
2-3 carrots (1 cup), coarsely chopped
1 leek (1 cup), coarsely chopped
½ stalk celery (½ cup), coarsely chopped
1 clove garlic
2 bay leaves
4 stalks parsley
10 peppercorns
2 sprigs fresh thyme or ½ tsp dried crushed thyme
2 tsp salt
12-14 cups cold water

Place chicken, onions, carrots, leek, and celery in a large stock pot. Add the garlic, bay leaves, parsley, peppercorns, thyme and salt. Cover all with cold water plus ¼ the depth (about 12-14 cups).
   Bring to the boil. Remove all scum very thoroughly. Lower heat to simmering point and continue cooking at this temperature for 3 hours.
   Strain carefully through two layers of rinsed cheesecloth. Stock will keep 1 week in the refrigerator, much longer frozen.

Cream Puff Paste

½ cup water
¼ tsp salt
¼ cup butter
½ cup all-purpose flour, sifted
2 eggs

Place the water in a heavy-bottomed saucepan. Put over high heat. As soon as it boils, add the salt and butter. Return to the boil. Add flour all at once, stirring and heating hard until the ingredients form a stiff ball that comes away from the sides of the pan. Remove from the heat. Transfer to the bowl of an electric mixer or beat in the saucepan. Add eggs, one at a time, beating well after each addition until the mixture is smooth and glossy.
   Pipe or drop from a spoon onto a greased baking sheet. This recipe will make 6 large puffs, 12 small puffs or fingers, or 18 tiny puffs.
   Bake at 425 degrees, 15 minutes for large puffs, 12 for small or fingers, 10 for the tiny puffs. Reduce heat to 375 degrees and bake till golden brown, about 25 minutes for the large puffs, 20 for the small or fingers, and 15 for the tiny puffs.
   Remove from the sheet. Cool on a rack. Split and remove any gummy dough remaining inside to keep the puffs crisp. Fill as desired.

Custard Sauce

2 cups milk
4 egg yolks
¼ cup white sugar
½ tsp salt
½ tsp vanilla

Scald the milk in the top of a double boiler over direct heat until little bubbles form around the edge. Beat together the egg yolks, sugar, and salt. Add ½ cup of the hot milk to the yolk mixture. Stir well. Strain back into the rest of the hot milk, blending well. Place over simmering water. Cook, stirring constantly, until thick enough to coat a spoon, 165 degrees. Add vanilla and cool, stirring several times. Serve in a jug.

Mayonnaise

2 egg yolks
1 tsp mild prepared mustard
1 tsp vinegar
½ tsp salt
⅛ tsp freshly ground white pepper
pinch of cayenne pepper
¼ cup olive oil
½ tsp lemon juice
¾ cup olive oil
½ tsp lemon juice
1 tbsp boiling water

All ingredients should be at room temperature.

Beat egg yolks until thick. Blend in mustard, vinegar, salt, white pepper, and cayenne pepper.

Add by drops the ¼ cup oil, beating continuously as the emulsification takes place. Use a wire whisk or a hand or electric beater. Add the first ½ tsp lemon juice and the rest of the olive oil in a trickle, beating continuously. Beat in the rest of the lemon juice and the boiling water.

Yield: about 1 cup.

Pie Crust (Flaky Pastry)

1 ¾ cups unsifted all-purpose flour
½ tsp salt
⅔ cup shortening
⅓ cup cold water

Place the flour and salt in a large mixing bowl. Work in the shortening, using a pastry blender or two knives until large loose crumbs the size of peas are formed. Sprinkle in the water, a tablespoonful or so at a time, using a fork to draw the moistened crumbs into a ball. Add no more water than is necessary to form the ball. Turn out on a lightly floured board. Quickly form dough into a ball with your hands. Divide into two pieces for 9" or 10" pie shells. Chill.

To prepare unfilled tart shells, prick the pastry with a fork and bake at 425 degrees for 8-10 minutes. Cool in the pan.

Yield: a double-crusted 9" or 10" pie or 2 bottom 9" or 10" pie shells or 18 medium tart shells.

Puff Pastry

4 ½ cups all-purpose flour
2 tsp salt
⅓ cup chilled butter
2 cups cold water
¾ cup all-purpose flour
2 ⅔ cups chilled butter

Sift the 4 ½ cups flour and salt into a large bowl. Blend in the ⅓ cup butter, using your hands. Stir in the water. The mixture will be very sticky. Turn out onto a board. Cut through the dough with your finger, pick up one half of the dough, and smack it down on the dough on the board. Repeat this cutting and smacking until the dough firms up, becomes elastic, and is no longer sticky. This usually takes about 5 minutes. Dust the board lightly with flour and form the dough on it into a smooth ball. Cut a cross ½" deep on the top of the ball. Cover with a large bowl and allow the dough to rest 15-20 minutes.

Pour the ¾ cup flour over the 2 ⅔ cups butter. Work the flour into the butter, but do not allow the butter to become smeary. Shape into a smooth square 7" x 7". Wrap in waxed paper and refrigerate 20 minutes.

Roll the dough into a square with rounded elongated corners. Keep centre of the dough twice as thick as the corners. Place the butter on the dough kitty-corner. Fold the corners of the dough over the butter, making sure that no air is trapped between the butter and the dough. Using a rolling pin and a firm hand, hit the dough 4 times vertically and 4 times horizontally.

Place the dough on a lightly floured piece of waxed paper, 24″ long. Roll out the dough to the length of the paper. Be careful in this and all the other rollings not to pierce the dough and let the butter break through.

Mentally divide the dough into 3 parts. Fold the right third over the middle and the left third over both the right and the middle thirds. Remove from the paper. Place on a piece of lightly floured waxed paper 18″ long. Roll out to this length. This time mentally divide the dough into 4 parts. Fold in the right and left quarters towards the middle, leaving a ½″ gap between them. Fold in half again, so that you can see the 4 layers. Wrap and refrigerate 30 minutes.

Repeat this rolling out and folding, first into thirds and then into quarters. Each time use an 18″ piece of lightly floured waxed paper. When rolling, use a light touch, brushing off excess flour as you work.

Divide the dough into 4 parts, wrap well, and refrigerate. This dough can be very successfully frozen and used later. Since effort and expense are involved in this kind of pastry, it is advisable to make it in large quantities and freeze it.

Pumpkin Purée

1 small pie pumpkin

Cut the pumpkin into 1″ slices. Remove the seeds and peel. Place in a steamer over boiling water and steam until tender, about 20-25 minutes. Remove and mash thoroughly, or pass through a food mill or push through a sieve. As one pumpkin makes more than enough purée for one dessert, freeze any that remains for future use. Canned pumpkin may be substituted for pumpkin purée.

Stone-ground Brown Bread

1 package active dry yeast (2 tsp)
1 tbsp brown sugar
½ cup warm water
¼ cup butter
½ cup firmly packed brown sugar
1 ½ tsp salt
2 ½ cups boiling water
1 well-beaten egg
3 ½ cups stone-ground whole wheat flour
½ cup wheat germ
3-4 cups unsifted all-purpose flour

Dissolve yeast and the 1 tbsp sugar in lukewarm water. Let stand 10 minutes.

Combine butter, ½ cup sugar, salt, and boiling water in a large bowl. Stir to melt butter. Cool to lukewarm. Add the beaten egg and the yeast mixture.

Beat in the whole wheat flour, the wheat germ, and 2 cups of the white flour. Turn dough out on a well-floured board and knead about 10 minutes, incorporating approximately another 2 cups of flour while kneading. The dough will be elastic and quite smooth. Form into a ball.

Place the dough in a large, greased mixing bowl. Turn the dough over to grease on all sides. Cover with a damp cloth and leave in a warm place to double in bulk, 1-1 ½ hours.

Punch down the dough. Roll the dough into a uniform log shape. Divide into 3 parts, using a sharp knife. Shape the ends and place each in a loaf tin. Cover lightly with a damp cloth and let rise until double in bulk, approximately 1 hour. Test by gently poking finger in dough. If hole remains, dough has risen enough.

Bake at 400 degrees 10 minutes, reduce heat to 375 degrees, and continue baking about 30-40 minutes. To test for doneness, remove a loaf from the oven and then from the tin. Tap. If the loaf sounds hollow it is ready. Remove all the loaves from the tins and cool on a rack. For a soft crust, brush loaves with melted butter after their removal from the oven.

Yield: three 9" x 5" loaves.

Toasted Slivered or Sliced Almonds

blanched almonds

Spread blanched slivered or sliced almonds on a baking sheet and place in an oven preheated to 325 degrees. Bake 2-3 minutes, stir, and continue baking 2-3 minutes more or until the almonds are lightly toasted. As almonds burn easily, care must be taken to watch and stir them.

Whipped Cream

1 cup heavy cream
1 tsp white sugar
a few grains of salt
1-2 drops vanilla

Chill the cream, beaters or whisk, and bowl until they are thoroughly cold. Beat or whisk the cream until it stands in soft peaks. Be careful not to overbeat or the cream will turn to butter. Unsweetened whipped cream is delicious for most desserts but if sweetened whipped cream is desired, stir the sugar, salt and vanilla into the whipped cream.

White Bread

1 package active dry yeast (2 tsp)
1 tsp white sugar
½ cup lukewarm water
2 tbsp butter
3 tbsp white sugar
1 tbsp salt
1 cup boiling water
1 cup milk
8 cups all-purpose flour

Dissolve yeast and 1 tsp sugar in lukewarm water. Let stand 10 minutes in a warm place.

Combine butter, 3 tbsp white sugar, salt, and boiling water in a large bowl. Stir to melt butter. Add milk and cool to lukewarm.

Add yeast mixture to the mixture in the large bowl. Beat in 4 cups of the flour, using an electric mixer. The batter should be smooth. Beat in 2 more cups by hand and turn out onto a well-floured board. Knead in as much of the last 2 cups as necessary to make an unsticky dough. Continue kneading 10 minutes in all or until the dough is smooth and elastic.

Put the dough in a greased bowl. Turn to grease all sides. Cover with a damp cloth and set in a warm place to rise until double in bulk, about 1 hour. A just-warmed oven is ideal.

Punch down the dough, divide in half, form into two loaves, and place in greased 9" x 5" loaf tins. Cover pans loosely with a damp cloth. Let rise until double in bulk, about 1 hour.

Bake 45 minutes at 375 degrees. For a crusty loaf, place a dish of warm water in the oven during the baking. The loaves are done when they sound hollow when tapped. Remove from tins and cool on a rack.

Definitions

Baste:

Basting is done during roasting in dry heat. To baste, periodically douse in pan drippings or melted butter or a sauce, as indicated. This seals the juices in the meat and improves its flavour. Meat well-marbled with fat and protected by an outer layer of fat does not need basting. Many of the recipes for roasting meats included in this book call for a seasoned (but not salty) fatty paste to be spread over the meat before roasting in dry heat. This paste seals the juices in the roast and helps create some initial basting fat. This is especially true for lean meats like tenderloin or the lean parts of roasts.

Broil:

Broiling means cooking food close to direct, very intense heat. Only one side at a time is exposed to the heat.

Cream:

This important step helps to create fine light cakes. It requires vigorous beating of the fat (usually butter or shortening) until it is light and fluffy. Sugar is gradually beaten into the fat until the mixture is very smooth and light.

Hull:

To *hull*, remove the outer shell or pod of a fruit or vegetable, or in the case of strawberries, remove the stem end.

Jam stage:

Put a china plate into the refrigerator when the jam begins to cook. As the jam thickens, remove the cold plate and drop a little jam onto the plate. Run a toothpick or a fork through the jam; if the jam wrinkles as you do this the jam stage has been reached. If the jam is too liquid for wrinkles to form, continue cooking and testing.

Knead:

To *knead* dough, place it on a lightly-floured board, press down firmly with the heels of both hands, turn the dough one quarter to the right, pull the far side of the dough over to the near, press again, turn and pull, and repeat the process rhythmically. This develops the gluten in the flour and creates a fine texture in the baked bread. Most breads are kneaded about 10 minutes and the dough becomes smooth and elastic; however, for some breads with a loose airy texture, little or no kneading is required.

Parboil:	To begin the cooking process by an initial boiling.
Punch down:	Make a fist and firmly punch the once-risen dough down in a greased bowl. Two or three punches are all that are necessary for the dough to return to its original size.
Purée:	Finely mashed or blended fruits, vegetables or meat.
Rasp:	To *rasp*, draw the sharp tines of a fork through the tender skin of fruit or vegetables. This is frequently done to cucumbers in order to create a decorative pattern on the edge of the slices.
Sauté:	To fry lightly over moderate heat.
Scald:	To *scald* milk or cream, heat over medium heat until little bubbles form around the edge of the saucepan. This generally occurs at about 180 degrees.
Sheet:	To test jelly for doneness, dip a metal spoon into the boiling jelly, and hold it horizontally over the jelly. Before the jelly is ready, the jelly flows rapidly in two streams off the spoon. As the jelly comes nearer to the jelling stage the two streams will come close to each other, until finally, at point of jelling, two drops will come into one off the middle of the spoon. As they do so they create a fairly wide, thin piece of jelly. This is sheeting.
Simmer:	To cook just below the boiling point.
Skewer:	To close the cavity and neck of poultry use sharp pins, skewers or needle and heavy thread.
Steam:	To cook over boiling water. This may be done in a steamer, or a container with a perforated bottom and a cover that fits neatly into a pot over boiling water. To steam a pudding, the pudding is placed right in the boiling water; the bottom of the pudding dish should rest on a small rack so that it does not come in direct contact with the bottom of the saucepan. The boiling water should come about ⅔ way up the side of the pudding dish and additional boiling water should be added when necessary to maintain the level.

Bibliography

Books

Acton, Eliza. *Modern Cooking for Private Families*. London, England: Elek Books Ltd., 1966. First published in London, England: Longman Brown, and Co., 1845.

Aitken, Kate. *Kate Aitken's Canadian Cook Book, Tamblyn Edition*. Toronto, Ontario: Wm. Collins Sons & Co. Ltd., 1950.

Assiniwi, Bernard. *Indian Recipes*. Toronto, Ontario: The Copp Clark Publishing Company, 1972.

Avon Chapter I.O.D.E., Stratford Ontario Cook Book. Stratford, Ontario: 1926

Beecher, Catharine E. *Miss Beecher's Domestic Receipt Book*. New York: Harper and Brothers, Publishers, 1854.

Beeton, Mrs. Isabella. *Beeton's Book of Household Management*. London, England: Jonathon Cape, 1968. First published in London, England: S.O. Beeton, 1861.

Benoit, Mme Jehane. *Encyclopedia of Canadian Cooking*. Winnipeg, Manitoba: Greywood Publishing Limited, 1970.

Berglund, Berndt and Bolsby, Clare E. *The Edible Wild*. Toronto, Ontario: Pagurian Press, 1971.

Boorman, Sylvia. *Wild Plums in Brandy*. New York: McGraw Hill, 1969.

Bowerman, Lucy. *The Canadian Cook Book. A Manual of Cookery and Domestic Economy*. Toronto, Ontario: The Toronto Graduate Nurses' Club, 1908.

Calvin Presbyterian Church, Winnipeg. Cook Book. Winnipeg, Manitoba: Calvin Presbyterian Church, Sunday Church School, 19??

The Canadian Home Cook Book. Compiled by Ladies of Toronto and Chief Cities and Towns in Canada. Toronto, Ontario: Ontario Reprint Press, 1970. First published by Hunter, Rose and Company, 1877.

Canadian Housewife's Manual of Cookery. Hamilton, Ontario: Henry J. Richards of the Spectator Office, 1861.

Canadian Mennonite Cookbook. Revised edition of the original *Altona Women's Institute Cookbook*. Toronto, Ontario: George J. McLeod, Limited, 1965.

Collett, Elaine. *The Chatelaine Cookbook*. Toronto, Ontario: Maclean-Hunter Limited, 1965.

The Cook Not Mad or Rational Cookery. Kingston, Ontario: James Macfarlane, 1831.

Denison, Grace E. (Lady Gay, pseud.) of *Saturday Night*. *The Canadian Family Cook Book*. Toronto, Ontario: McLeod & Allen, 1914.

East York Schools Win-The-War Cook Book. Toronto, Ontario: The East York Schools Win-The-War Fund Committee, 194?.

Favorite Recipes 1930-1931. Compiled by the Women's Institute of Tillsonburg, Ontario, 1931.

Five Roses Cook Book. Montreal, P.Q.: Lake of the Woods Milling Company Limited, 1915.

Food-à la canadienne. Ottawa, Canada: Food Advisory Services. Canada Department of Agriculture, 1970.

Gaertner, Erika E. *Harvest Without Planting*. Chalk River, Ontario, 1967.

Gougeon, Helen. *Helen Gougeon's Good Food*. Toronto, Ontario: The Macmillan Company of Canada Limited, 1958.

Group Cook Book. Group 2 Women's Association of Foxboro United Church, 1955.

A Guide to Good Cooking Compiled by the Makers of Five Roses Flour. Compiled under the supervision of Jean Brodie. Montreal-Winnipeg: Lake of the Woods Milling Company Limited, 1938.

A Guide to Good Cooking with Five Roses Flour, Being a Collection of Good Recipes. Carefully tested and approved under supervision of Pauline Harvey. Montreal-Winnipeg: Lake of the Woods Milling Company, Limited, 1962.

Handbook of Practical Cookery, for the use of Household Science Classes in the Public Schools of Toronto. Toronto, Ontario: Board of Education, 191?.

Horst, Mary Ann. *Pennsylvania Dutch Fun, Folklore and Cooking*. Kitchener, Ontario: Pennsylvania Dutch Craft Shop, 19??.

The Laura Secord Canadian Cook Book. Prepared by the Canadian Home Economics Association. Toronto/Montreal: McClelland and Stewart Limited, 1966.

MacIlquham, Frances. *Canadian Game Cookery*. Toronto/Montreal: McClelland and Stewart Limited, 1966.

The Metropolitan Cook Book. Ottawa, Canada: Metropolitan Life Insurance Company, 192?.

Moffat Cook Book. The Moffat Stove Company, 194?.

1964 Cook Book. Fullarton, Ontario: Fullerton Women's Institute, 1964.

Northern Cookbook. Edited by Eleanor A. Ellis. Ottawa, Canada: Issued Under the Authority of the Honourable Arthur Laing, P.C., M.P., B.S.A. Minister of Indian Affairs and Northern Development, Information Canada, 1967.

Nourse, Mrs. *Modern Cookery*. Montreal, P.Q.: Armour & Ramsay, 1845.

"Our Best" an Indispensible Cook Book. Compiled by the ladies of Grace Church Sewing Circle. Brantford, Ontario: Donovan & Henwood, 1900.

Our Family Favorites. Gathered by Shining Star Chapter 293 O.E.S. Mitchell, Ontario. Mitchell, Ontario: 1967.

Pattinson, Nellie Lyle. *Canadian Cook Book*. Toronto, Ontario: The Ryerson Press, 1930.

Pattinson, Nellie Lyle. *Nellie Lyle Pattinson's Canadian Cook Book*. Revised by Helen Wattie and Elinor Donaldson. Toronto, Ontario: Ryerson Press McGraw-Hill Company of Canada Limited, 1969.

Read, Jessie. *Three Meals a Day*. Toronto, Ontario: The Musson Book Company Ltd., 1941.

Sebringville Ontario Favorite Recipes. Compiled by the Helping Hands Class, Emmanuel Church, Sebringville, Ontario: 1957.

Spice Flavoured Canadian Recipes. The Canadian Spice Association, 19??.

Staebler, Edna. *Food that Really Schmecks.* Toronto, Ontario: Ryerson Press McGraw-Hill Company of Canada, Limited, 1969.

Taylor, Margaret and McNaught, Frances. *The New Galt Cook Book.* Toronto, Ontario: George J. McLeod, Limited, 1898.

Handwritten personal recipe collections	Anonymous Receipt Book, Baldwin Room, Toronto Public Library. Toronto, Ontario, 183?-184?.
	Baird, Elizabeth and Baird, Margaret. Plattsville and Toronto, Ontario, 1900-1960.
	Fisken, Mrs. John. Toronto, Ontario, 1856-?.
	Forbes, Hugh. Toronto, Ontario, 1936-1937.
	Haslett, Jean. Hamilton, Ontario, 1905-mid 1960s.
	Haslett, Mary. Hamilton, Ontario, 1912-late 1950s.
	Haslett, Rachel C. Hamilton, Ontario, 1884-1919.
	Kittson, Meredith H. Hamilton, Ontario, 1880-?.
	Morris, Janey. Fullarton, Ontario, 1900-1940.
	The Parker family. Uxbridge, Ontario, dating from the 1880s.

Pamphlets *Canada Department of Agriculture*	*Apples* # 1402, 1970.
	Beans (revised) #1141, 1970.
	Cheese # 1396, 1969.
	Festive Foods #1407, Christmas 1972.
	Home Canning of Fruits and Vegetables #789, 1965.
	Home preparation of juices, wines & cider #1406, 1970.
	How to Buy/How to Cook Poultry #1189, 1964.
	Jams Jellies and Pickles #992, 1956.
	Let's barbecue #1443, 1971.
	Maple Syrup Sugar Butter Taffy #1096, 1961.
	Meat #971, 1956, revised 1971.
	Potatoes (revised) #1058, 1971.
	Pork #1428, 1970.
	Squash and Pumpkin #1140, 1968.
	Summer Vegetables #1130, 1962.
	Using Savory Herbs #1374, 1968.

Department of Fisheries of Canada	Favourite Fish Recipes Cat. No. Fs 32-7/1962.
	Let's Serve Freshwater Fish Cat. No. Fs 32-20/1963.

Dominion of Canada- Department of Agriculture	Wartime Canning Jams and Jellies #751, May 1943.

Index

Included in this index is a guide to recipes which are particularly time-consuming to prepare (indicated with a *), recipes which can be made in advance (indicated by a † sign), and recipes which are quick and easy (indicated by a ° sign).

* = time-consuming recipe
† = can be made in advance
° = quick and easy recipe